D0605392

Early Praise for *ONE Team*

"Organizational success requires a one-team mentality. This book provides a practical approach to creating the culture required to build and develop successful leadership teams."
–Patrick Criteser, President & CEO, Tillamook

"This book is an advanced course on how to ask effective questions to achieve exceptional outcomes – and develop an inspired workforce."
–David Yates, Regional Business Head, North America, Nestlé Health Science

"Only inspired teams can achieve the extraordinary. Craig and Angie provide an essential framework to guide leaders and their teams to the extraordinary, where magic exists."
–Lance Secretan, author of *The Spark, The Flame and The Torch*

"We continue to elevate our business performance. There's no question: The tools in *ONE Team* are a game and life changer!"
–Phil Horlock, President and CEO, Blue Bird Corporation

"*ONE Team* aligns perfectly with our cultural approach, and equips us to get the most out of every interaction. The outcome is a winning, can-do attitude that is infectious, inspiring us to tackle our toughest business challenges effectively."
–Kevin McEvoy, President & CEO, Oceaneering

"Ross and Paccione's passion for culture in the workplace is captured with his uncanny sense of building leadership and delivering a greater purpose through practical and meaningful conversations, using key performance points to deliver powerful results."
–Scott Teepe, Sr., President & CEO, TP Mechanical Contractors

"We're implementing 21st century education. To do that, we need 21st century leadership. This book is 21st century leadership."
–Dr. James Calhoun, Principal, Castle View High School

ALSO BY CRAIG W. ROSS:

Degrees of Strength

Craig W. Ross & Steven W. Vannoy, 2012 Wister & Willows

Best Books Award Finalist, USA Book News I Silver Axiom Business Book Award

www.degreesofstrength.com

Stomp the Elephant in the Office

Steven W. Vannoy & Craig W. Ross, 2008 Wister & Willows

Best Books Award Finalist, USA Book News

www.stomptheelephant.com

ONE
TEAM

10-Minute Discussions That Activate Inspired Teamwork

Craig W. Ross & Angela V. Paccione, Ph.D.

Verus Global Leadership Press
10822 West Toller Drive, Suite 300
Littleton, CO 80127
www.verusglobal.com

Library of Congress Control Number 2014955763

ONE Team : 10-minute discussions that activate inspired teamwork / Craig W. Ross and
        Angela V. Paccione, Ph. D.

ISBN 978-0-9793768-3-2
1. Leadership. I. Title
2014955763

THIS BOOK IS DEDICATED

TO PEOPLE WHO BELIEVE
THEIR TEAM CAN
ACCOMPLISH MORE –
**AND HAVE THE COURAGE TO
DO SOMETHING ABOUT IT.**

**No one can whistle a symphony.
It takes a whole orchestra to play it.**
– H.E. Luccock

CONTENTS

A Note To The Reader... 1

Prologue: Defining One Team

It Is Time To Act..3
The Anti-Productivity Forces...4
ONE Team Is Different 6
One Team Quickly...7
A Note To Skeptics 9
One Team Begins...11

Introduction: Why Inspired Teamwork Matters

Inspire Others To Act Differently..13
Rearrange Thinking 15
Okay, You're Not Kennedy...17
The Duty Of Each Team Member 18
Two Questions Your Team Must Ask 19
Putting This Book To Work 20
An Important Caution 21

Chapter One: What The One-Team Approach Looks Like

Big Trouble 25
De-Activating Teamwork 25
It Happens Everywhere 26
It's Not How Smart You Are 27
What Predicts Your Team's Success 28
Results Never Lie 32
Amplify Your Input 33

Chapter Two: How To Activate Inspired Teamwork

Move Your World...35
Long Lever Questions 36
Do You Know This Person? 37
A Boss Becomes A Leader...40
Words = Direction 44
Un-activated Teammates 45

Chapter Three: Use Your Power To Elevate Performance

Eliminate Your Team's Final Barrier...49
Power Over People = Performance Barriers 52
You Have New Status: Step Up, Speak Out, And Lead............54
Establish A New Pattern Of Communication 55
Do You Believe? 57
Activate Inspired Teamwork 59

Chapter Four:
Developing
One-Team
Awareness

EXECUTION – The Dangers Of Intellectual Sex 63
HONESTY – Are You "Nice" Or "Professional?" 65
CULTURE – This Is A Condition Of Your Employment 67
TEAMWORK – Is Your "Team Technology" Outdated? 69
TRANSPARENCY – The Antidote To Communication Competition ..71
IDENTITY – What Your Customer Doesn't Care About 73
INCLUSION – Why Are You Invited To Meetings? 75
EMPATHY – Making Sure Families Get More Than "Leftovers" 77
TALENT – The War For Problem Talent 79
LEARN – The Most Important Decision Of A Career 81
LEGACY – You Can't Buy This – But Need It 83
Chapter Four Summary 85
One Team Progress Assessment 88
Successes From The Field: Long Lever Questions In Action 89
Developing The Skill Of Using Long Lever Questions 92

Chapter Five:
Creating
One-Team
Alignment

PERSEVERANCE – The Mindset For High Performance 99
INNOVATION – If You Have This Instinct, Trust It 101
COURAGE – Why Wimps Shouldn't Be Blamed For Not Speaking Out ..103
LEADERSHIP – Mr. Fix-It And His Fatal Mistake 105
EMPOWERMENT – The World's (un)Luckiest Employee 107
RISK TAKING – When Playing It Safe Hurts 109
VISION – I Blowed It Up 111
MOMENTUM – Free Gas For Life 113
INITIATIVE – What Are You Waiting For? 115
RESPECT – What Will You Do When You're A Target? 117
Chapter Five Summary 119
One Team Progress Assessment 122
Developing The Skill Of Using Long Lever Questions 123

Chapter Six:
Driving
One-Team
Actions

FOCUS – The Discipline Of Teaming Forward 127
COMMUNICATION – The High-Performance Discussion 129
COLLABORATION – Is Your Approach What's Best For Results? 131
STRATEGY – What If "What If" Happens? 133
ALIGNMENT – What's In Your Future: A Collision Or "One Team"? ...135
AGILITY – What It Takes To Be An Agility-Ready Team 137
KNOWLEDGE – Date Rich, Knowledge Poor 139
VALUES – Beware The Team Hijacker 141
INTEGRITY – A Call For A Certain Courage 143
QUALITY – It Happens When You Elevate The Reason 145
Chapter Six Summary 147
One Team Progress Assessment 150
Successes From The Field 151
Developing The Skill Of Using Long Lever Questions 155

Chapter Seven:
Accomplishing
One-Team
Accountability

TIME MANAGEMENT – It's Not The Time, It's The Performance Paradigm...161
DISCIPLINE – Delivering Consequences To Learn Success..........163
EMPOWERMENT – Cream Or Crud: What's Elevated In Your Organization?..165
CHANGE – How To Support Peers Through Change 167
ACCOUNTABILITY – The Perfect Team To Succeed........................169
LOYALTY – Getting Friendships Right...171
REFUSAL – One Word To Achieve More: No 173
COMMITMENT – Does The Competition Fear You? 175
ENDURANCE – What It Takes To Be A Legend................................177
MOTIVATION – Don't Be The Reason Your Team Fails....................179
Chapter Seven Summary 181
One Team Progress Assessment...183
Developing The Skill Of Using Long Lever Questions 184

Chapter Eight:
Activating
One-Team
Inspiration

PRIDE – What Causes Us To Give More...189
GROWTH – What Are You In The Business Of Doing? 191
PARTNERSHIPS – Where Are The Borders For Your Team? 193
EXCELLENCE – The Michelangelo Approach To High Performance.195
PROACTIVE – Four Categories Of Questions That Facilitate Change....197
DIVERSITY – After We're Done Criticizing Each Other 199
INSPIRATION – The Human Spirit Was Not Meant To Conform ... 201
ENGAGEMENT- Do Bonuses Increase Engagement (If Not, What Does?).203
FEEDBACK – How To Amplify Excellence 205
CELEBRATION – The Loser Syndrome And Its Cost........................207
TRUST – Don't Apologize 209
Chapter Eight Summary 211
One Team Progress Assessment...214
Successes From The Field 215
Developing The Skill Of Using Long Lever Questions 218

Chapter Nine:
What We Are
Capable Of
Achieving
Together

What Sort Of Influence Will You Apply?... 229
Predict Discoveries For Your Team 229
Look Up.. 230
Change The Discussion The World Is Having 232

Appendices

Appendix A: Bonus Material 234
    LEADING UP – Only For Teams With Guts 235
    BALANCE – When PTO = Pretend Time Off 237
    SYSTEMS – What You Can't See Can Limit You 239
    CONSISTENCY – The Habits Of Excellence 241
Appendix B: Long Lever Questions Feedback Form.......................245
Acknowledgments 246
Bibliography & Notes 248
Index.. 252

A NOTE TO THE READER:

The text within this book is written in the combined voice of Craig Ross and Angie Paccione. It is important to emphasize, however, that the work this book represents is the effort of the entire team at Verus Global, and we give full credit to these individuals at the conclusion of this book. It is the collective experiences of lives and work done on six continents that forms the wisdom in these pages. While it is the honor of Craig and Angie to arrange the delivery of this content, the credit belongs to the team.

In those rare cases when "I" is used within the text it is done for reader simplicity, content flow, or because the reference to Ross or Paccione is important for understanding or comprehension.

Also, in some cases, we've changed the names of the leaders whose stories are shared within these pages. Regardless, their stories are true and inspiring.

Defining One Team

It Is Time To Act

Legendary Hall of Fame baseball manager Casey Stengel said, "Gettin' good players is easy. Gettin' 'em to play as a team is another story."[1] Given that organizations everywhere are filled with loosely aligned groups of talented people falling painfully short of their collective potential, Stengel was right:

Activating inspired teamwork is a distinct and essential skill.

If you've ever walked out of a meeting and muttered, "This team could do so much more," then searched for a mechanism to activate inspired teamwork, this book is for you. It's a research-supported solution for any person who, like Stengel, passionately believes in the power of collective effort and is seeking ways to make it a daily reality.

We promise: During the first 10 minutes of your next meeting, you can inspire and develop a more productive team. And you don't even need to be the meeting leader. We're that confident. We've seen the results too many times not to be. (To the skeptics: There's a note for you near the end of this Prologue.)

Nearly all the professionals we've ever met, in every organization, want to be a part of something bigger than themselves. They want to contribute to a movement that achieves extraordinary things. But this book isn't for those who merely harbor this motivation. Evidence shows not all people have the skills to *act* in ways that are consistent with their values. The hard-hitting pages that follow are for those who are ready to *do*, who can see what their team can become – and want to develop greater skills to get there fast.

We don't care what role you have in the organization, whether or not you went to college, or what level of "status" you've achieved. The idea that any of us should wait for the "leader" of the team to create the dynamics essential for high performance is a costly and destructive belief. Organizations are filled with people who are waiting. It's time we all step up, speak out, and activate inspired teamwork.

The Anti-Productivity Forces

Every team has limits in what it can achieve. Why do some have ceilings of performance that are lower than others? The research, revealed in *ONE Team*, on why many teams consistently underperform, as well as what best predicts how well a team will achieve, may surprise you.

A primary reason, for example: One or more team members think they're using forms of power for the benefit of the team. In reality, though, the power is used over others, rather than for others and in service to the team. (And misuse of power isn't reserved just for those at the head of the table.) Such teams suffer these and other symptoms:

A. An incessant need by a few to make the majority of decisions
B. Daily discussions where participation is not equally distributed
C. Information that is purposefully or systemically restricted
D. Hidden agendas
E. The "I have more time at this company than you" dynamic
F. Teammates who rationalize a resistance to change
G. Average to low levels of expressed empathy by some toward others

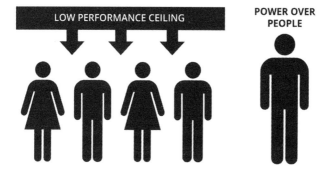

Incredibly, most team members are aware there are counterproductive forces restricting the growth and achievement of their team. Yet, they either believe they are powerless to do anything about it or they don't know how to overcome the behaviors and activate the greater potential within their team.

It's wrong for organizations to be denied productivity levels they could claim if the teams under their direction were more functional. More so, it's insulting to those who devote lives to careers only to retire with just a few memories of inspired and functional teamwork.

This book, with the tool it shares and the leaders and teams highlighted as evidence of its power, equips you to play a greater role in elevating the ceiling of performance for your team.

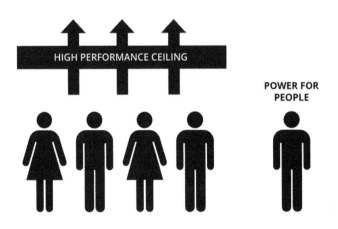

ONE Team Is Different

If you want a better machine, you buy one (or fix the one you have). If it's a leaner operation you desire, you study the data to reduce waste. But if you want to elevate team performance? Breakthrough solutions aren't found in the spreadsheets. Regardless of how often we hear it, we passionately reject the idea that people are "cogs in a machine." (No joke. Some people still make this claim.) People and teams are not instruments intended for cold manipulation; therefore, they shouldn't be treated as such.

Activating the full potential of a team isn't accomplished or sustained when people pontificate, reorganize, demand, cut, reward, punish, travel to the occasional ropes course, or cross their fingers. While some of those techniques influence one-team dynamics, to inspire any team to elevated performance requires one thing to happen: It must be the *team's idea* to come together as one.

The most effective method to ensure an individual or team owns anything is to ensure they are a part of its creation. Nothing achieves this like the powerful tool presented in *ONE Team*. It's a particular type of question research shows few are asking, despite the fact that when it's used, it has a dramatic effect on the quality of teamwork necessary to break any performance ceilings.

There are a lot of books on teamwork, as well as the topic of asking questions and their subsequent effectiveness in achieving improved performance. *ONE Team* is different. It's for those who want improved results faster. Rather than making the thrust of this book about the technique of asking questions, this book provides you with the template you need to put the skill into immediate action.

One Team Quickly
ONE Team quickly activates the wisdom and better actions within your team.

Ten minutes into your next meeting you can create the dialogue research shows is necessary for your team to benefit from improved one-team performance.

Your team's 10-minute discussions come in the form of Activation Points. These points focus on specific behavioral competencies essential to improving teamwork. The competencies, selected from top organizations worldwide, are expressed in get-to-the-point-quick essays that will prompt your team to say, "It's about time we talked about the real issues."

The collective awareness your team will establish in minutes then serves as the "fulcrum," the pivot point of wisdom from which a subsequent, recommended, and strategic question will derive its strength. Here's what it looks like:

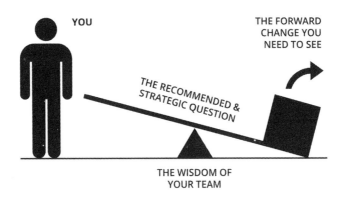

In moments, you will be prepared to inspire the conversation your team has been waiting to have (with destructive impatience, in some cases) and which is needed to influence change. Want to quickly create greater collaboration among your peers? Need to have higher levels of trust in order for your team to realize its potential? Use the table of contents to find the one-team behavior you most desire, and use the fulcrum and tailored questions on the corresponding pages to facilitate and influence quicker change.

By systematizing the approach of infusing these 10-minute discussions into weekly practice, as our most successful clients do, we promise you'll see sustained and enduring momentum in discovering what your team can achieve – without having to spend an additional minute on other techniques.

A Note To Skeptics

You might be thinking, "Ten minutes? The creation of 'one team?' That's impossible."

We welcome the skepticism. Frankly speaking, we don't blame you for doubting the promise. Here's why: There are no shortcuts to excellence. Additionally, using the tools and approach in this book doesn't mean a team will find itself transformed in minutes, everyone holding hands and singing the same song. In fact, that's not the definition of "one team."

This is the definition of one team:
Two or more people, who may have different responsibilities or find themselves separated by circumstances, yet are united in focus and purpose, and whose collective actions deliver different and greater performance than would otherwise be accomplished by individuals who only share common tasks, objectives, or other work.

Members of this particular type of team function in a progressively inspired state as a result of the collaborative partnering with their peers. When optimized, members of the team associate so strongly with the identity of the whole that they willingly, and often unconditionally, contribute efforts beyond those expected or ordinary. Ultimately, the benefit of this approach is excellence in delivery on the purpose of the team, as well as extraordinary intrinsic value for its membership.

It would be irresponsible to believe that a group of individuals could form and then perform at this defined level within 10 minutes.[2] It is, however, equally negligent to belong to any team and not consistently make efforts to develop and optimize the efforts of that team to this end. Ultimately, it's about a team's continuous improvement.

The have-to-go-faster world we all live in now is having a dangerous effect on employee and team development. Too many organizations claim they "don't have time" to improve team effectiveness. It doesn't take a genius to know the devastating effects such a philosophy has on business results.

The claims of the don't-have-time assembly and the can't-be-done-in-minutes group are appreciated, yet present opportunities for further discovery. Talent development – be it individual or collective – is much different today than it was just a few years ago. It is no longer adequate to rely on an event-based approach to team improvement (meaning the team participates in a one-day off-site training program and then goes back to work) for three specific reasons:

1. What a team must accomplish changes rapidly. Therefore, how a team functions together – or team competencies – must also change and develop with those needs. Teamwork is not static, nor should its development be so.

2. Time is in higher demand. Therefore, it is essential that an emphasis be placed on leveraging daily interactions as the mechanism for development.

3. "Team" is defined differently than it was before. Gone are the days when you spent your time with the same people, sitting in the same room, building, or even on the same continent. Now, members of teams, and their locations, interchange rapidly. As well, employees find themselves on several teams at once, based upon multiple responsibilities – yet all these employees are a part of one grander team.

As we've supported organizations of all sizes while they effectively address these dynamics (as this book does), we consistently see remarkable results.

One Team Begins

If an organization has employees grouped together who are not mentoring, teaching, directing, facilitating, or coaching – in other words, consistently activating the potential around them – as they move through the workday, the company is already at a considerable disadvantage. They can't hire and retain talent fast enough to keep pace: Talented people grouped together, but not equipped to activate the potential within each other, suddenly become quite average (at best) in their performance.

In order to succeed, today's organizations must have systems that strengthen individuals and teams as they do their work.

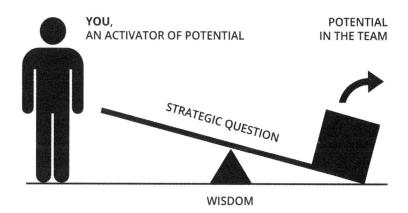

YOU,
AN ACTIVATOR OF POTENTIAL

POTENTIAL
IN THE TEAM

STRATEGIC QUESTION

WISDOM

From thousands of hours of experience, we know this for certain: Within 10 minutes your team can have the discussions it needs to have to elevate its performance effectiveness. Regardless of whether it's transformative or incremental steps that are made, it's the direction that is most important. For if a team is not working on improving itself, what is it becoming?

With each turn of the page, *ONE Team* will activate an inspired power that is unique to the team of which you are a part. And with this comes the achievement of your team's immense potential.

For videos and resources that compliment *ONE Team*,
and to support your team, visit
http://oneteambook.com/team

Why Inspired Teamwork Matters

Inspire Others To Act Differently

From your position on the team, how do you bring people together to function as one inspired team – in minutes – so they can achieve what has never been done before?

On January 20, 1961, newly elected United States President John F. Kennedy inspired millions of people to think and act differently. In his inaugural address he stated, "Ask not what your country can do for you; ask what you can do for your country."

With those words Kennedy planted a question that grew into a movement. It was a question that set a focus, brought a majority of Americans together, and energized people to perform at levels previously unachieved. Consequently, Kennedy prompted some of the most transformative changes in history – among them, important civil rights would be expanded, a generation of young Americans were inspired to join the Peace Corps Kennedy created, and man stepped onto the moon.

Can you imagine if Kennedy had scrapped his script and stated, "Here's what you have to do to make our world better." Such a statement would have only created more of the same: the world as it was before he was elected.

President Kennedy shifted the focus from "me" to "we." He knew what all great leaders of change know:

Deep inside every person is a fundamental desire to do good things – and not just for him- or herself, but for collective well-being.

Leaders quickly differentiate themselves when they act on this wisdom, because too few in the world of business remember to do so. Or, they don't know how.

Instead of business as usual, Kennedy elevated thinking. Rather than lecturing about potential, he activated it by planting a question that inspired a change of focus. What will you do for your country? This opened minds to new possibilities that were previously unimagined.

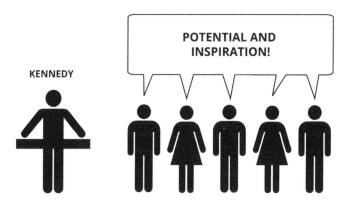

Rearrange Thinking

Try this experiment: Ask someone next to you a question, and then watch what happens to that person's focus. Observe any shifts exhibited in the person's energy.

You can safely predict that your unsuspecting bystander at least briefly shifted his or her focus. The reason: Questions trigger the mind. They activate new or different thinking. And it works nearly every time! Our gray matter can't resist it: Ask any question and – bammmm! – human beings seek the answer. Depending on what type of question you asked, you may have even noticed a sustained change in the person's thoughts and energy. This wisdom is profoundly important, and profoundly underutilized in influencing others: The right question changes behaviors.

It's likely you already knew the effectiveness of good questions long before you began reading this. What's not as likely is that you've observed leaders around you asking effective questions so you can talk about what needs to be addressed in your business. Now, we promise you that within the first 10 minutes in any meeting or interaction, regardless of your position on the team, you can use your wisdom to rearrange thinking and inspire high-performance teamwork.

To accomplish dramatic changes, Kennedy didn't tell citizens what to do for their country. He certainly didn't demand that they simply work harder. What he *did* do was rearrange thinking. He moved the view of our world. Asking the right question opens and lifts the mind from what is – to what can be. The more the question taps into a greater and common purpose, the more leverage it has. This develops the capacity your team has for excellence *together*.

By prompting a particular question at the right time, President Kennedy caused predictable outcomes to occur, all of which are identical to what organizations are in desperate need of today. The question:

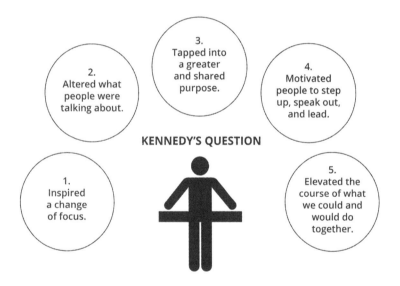

Kennedy did what leadership expert Warren Bennis said a good leader must do if the team is to succeed: Make people feel that they're at the very heart of things, not at the periphery.[3] This is the core of activating one-team performance. When people are at the "heart of things," it enables team members to perform with levels of inspired, collaborative determination.

Okay, You're Not Kennedy

Few of us will ever be in a position of grand influence like Kennedy's. Yet, just because you may not possess the power of presidents, CEOs, and other organizational executives, does that require you to submit your team to a fate untouched by you? We emphatically argue no. The number of boxes under your name on an organizational personnel chart is not related to the level of responsibility you have to bring your best effort to the team.

What are the consequences if your team fails? What would be the significance if every team in the organization only maintained its current level of productivity? Such questions can be useful, as they get teams past the focus on corporate performance targets – to a conversation about home foreclosures, college tuitions unpaid, families pulled apart, and personal health problems.

Inspired teamwork matters. It matters to children, marriages, communities, and our own fulfillment. There is urgency in developing the skill of functioning as one team that eclipses the needs of the boss or the desire to score well on the next performance review. To embrace the responsibility we each have to contributing to the success of the team is an act of immeasurable service.

Consider Kim, in her 20s and new to a team within the health care industry. With no one reporting to her, and several she's responsible to, she found herself in a project meeting where tension was rising. She had an idea, but who was she – a newcomer! – to speak up? Plus, she hadn't learned the cultural norms of what was acceptable and what was off limits for new employees. But she did know this: Her responsibility was to deliver value.

Kim cleared her throat and said, "I don't know what you guys know, and I'm eager to learn, so I can't help wondering: When we've been in similar situations with customers in the past, what have we learned the customer must see from us – that is also directly aligned with our value promise?" The results of the meeting were immediately enhanced. "This type of question," Kim reported later, "immediately expanded the vigorous debate – but now with a focus on the discovery of solutions. I certainly didn't come up with the action steps we outlined. But I feel good about the win I helped inspire."

The Duty Of Each Team Member

Whatever our position on the team we should never relinquish our role – our duty – to activate the greatness in others. **As a member of any team we only realize our individual potential when we successfully contribute to the effectiveness of the whole.** An aligned, coordinated team with a common focus will always outperform a group of unallied individuals. Develop a team that regularly functions with this wisdom and you achieve the extraordinary.

It's staggering how few organizations make developing inspired teamwork a priority. Consequently, they suffer not only poor results, but harbor workplaces where individuals feel marginalized.

In your next meeting you can start, transform, or accelerate the quality of teamwork. The proven wisdom and practices in this book will equip you to better deliver your responsibilities as a team member – as well as get you closer to any job you want to have on the team. By using the principles in *ONE Team*, you will also be able to answer these questions: How do I more effectively lead those who lead me? and How do I create a more satisfying experience while being a member of this team?

There is urgency in this matter. Team achievement – indeed, personal fulfillment – is at stake. Activate your team's potential by inspiring others to think and act differently. Do so with a particular type of question that moves their world.

If you had 2,400 minutes to spend, would you be willing to invest a mere 10 of those minutes if it meant your team was healthier, stronger, and further equipped to deliver excellence?

The sum 2,400 is how many minutes your team has in a 40-hour workweek. While most professionals find it laughable that a workweek be expressed in 40 hours, we maintain the number so as to be intentionally conservative regarding both what is required of you, as well as the benefits your team will receive. By investing a small fraction of the time you have, you can build something great.

If it meant your team was stronger, would you invest this time?

The 52 Activation Points in *ONE Team* provide you and your team with a yearlong framework to activate inspired teamwork. If your team chooses to move through the points sequentially, we encourage your team to ask these two questions and share responses prior to beginning:

1. **Why is it important to each of us that we develop inspired teamwork?**

2. **As we move through the next 12 months, how will we know we're successful in developing a one-team approach?**

As you move through the year, rather than a "check the box" exercise, we suggest you regularly assess your progress against the answers your team provides to these two questions. We know from experience that you will see your team make the important progress you envision.

To assist in your team's journey, we've broken the Activation Points into five chapters – four through eight. At the conclusion of each chapter we'll provide:

1. A summary of the "Big Ideas" covered in the preceding chapter.

2. A team assessment you can use to measure your progress against the answers formulated to the above two questions.

3. Periodic "Successes from the Field," which show additional real-life examples of what the tools look like in action.

4. Instructional segments that equip your team with the "how to" so they can further activate improved performance based upon the content in *ONE Team*.

Putting This Book To Work

The sequence of the Activation Points, while deliberate and proven to accomplish the results you desire, is not arranged or weighted in relation to importance. (Otherwise the topic of "trust" would not be the last Activation Point.) That said, the order of the Activation Points is of less consequence than the development needs of your team. Therefore, it might be best for your team to consider these alternative methods for using *ONE Team*:

A. What do organizational surveys tell you are the greatest behavioral development needs of your team? Use this data to design the course your team will take through the Activation Points. If surveys indicate you need greater trust among team members, for example, then begin with those related Activation Points.

B. If formal surveys are not available to you, create your own assessment. (These can be even more powerful than the formal.) Ask your team to answer the following questions, either individually or collectively, anonymously or publicly, then use their answers to chart your course through the Activation Points:

    a. As it relates to behavioral competencies, what are our greatest strengths as a team?

    b. In terms of our interactions with one another, what behaviors should we target for future development opportunities?

    c. What are specific reasons why we should invest in developing more effective, inspired teamwork?

C. Individual accountability to developing the strength of the team is a powerful dynamic. You can foster this by rotating responsibility among team members: Each week it's a different person's obligation to bring to the team the Activation Point of his or her choosing and share the rationale of that choice in advance of any discussion.

An Important Caution

Over the past 20 years our organization has taken on the audacious task of equipping teams to *sustain* extraordinary levels of achievement. We climb high peaks (and enter a few toxic arenas), stumble sleep-deprived through airports on six continents, endure knee-crushing seats on crowded planes, and get home long after our loved ones have gone to bed. And we do it for one reason: We are obsessed with our mission of equipping contributors at all levels of an organization to better put individual and organizational values into action. When people do so, they realize their brilliant potential.

No surprise, we've observed teams in dire straits, and then had the thrill of celebrating with them when they've delivered results greater than they thought they could. *ONE Team* brings you the insights and wisdom these leaders and teams have revealed to us in their journev.

Before we begin, though, three points of caution:

1. The topics covered in the Activation Points are rich in content, making it tempting to devour all of them in one sitting. However, the unique questions that follow each point provide the how to activate one-team performance. We encourage you to do the same thing we have leaders in the field do: *Ask the questions and allow your team to answer.* Be purposeful: Your objective is not to show how smart you are; what you're after is one aligned, focused, high-performing team. A question is only as valuable as the level of ability demonstrated in effectively listening and hearing the response.

2. Asking questions requires people to think. This is an exercise many teams, indeed entire work cultures, have been trained for generations to not do. The human brain, if not self-aware, seeks the path of least resistance. Translation: Too many people are waiting to be told what to do. On the surface, such an approach appears easier. But one day into executing any project and it becomes painfully evident: Your team's success depends on people thinking, anticipating, and acting on their own in a manner that's accountable to the whole. In other words, when you ask the unique questions in this book, don't be surprised if initially there's silence in the room or on the phone. Your patience, your determination to hold to the belief that the team is stronger than any individual, will pay off. With increased frequency, the team will respond: They will think, which means you will have begun to activate more effective actions.

3. Thousands of years of conditioning have taught all of us that leadership is a function of the position a person holds. Yet, there's enough research now to confirm what most of us intuitively know: Successful teams are composed of individuals who embrace and lead their area of responsibility. Each employee is a leader: All are leaders of self; some are leaders of teams and projects; a few are leaders of the business. Regardless of the role, everyone influences the effectiveness of the team. Indeed, everyone *should* and must if the team is to succeed. We've observed leaders everywhere in all types of roles and situations who use the wisdom in this book to activate their team's potential. As you read, you'll often see the word "leader." Know that we're addressing everyone, and leaving it to you to determine the unique application of the content as it relates to your role.

Get ready.
This book is an accelerant.

You're about to use a proven approach to strengthen your influence – and activate the potential with those whom you are teamed. The result will be the discovery of what only one team can achieve.

History proves far too few people consistenly unify a team's efforts effectively.

CHAPTER ONE:

What The One-Team Approach Looks Like

Big Trouble

Ford seemed doomed. Everyone knew the automobile manufacturer was in trouble.[1] The numbers were staggering and scary: Since 1990, Ford had lost 25 percent of its market share, and in 2006 they were preparing to post the largest annual loss in its 103-year history: $12.7 billion.[2,3] Bankruptcy was a forgone conclusion by many of the world's financial experts.[4]

"We've been going out of business for 40 years," the new CEO, Alan Mulally, told employees after taking the helm in 2006.

But Alan Mulally wasn't about to let that happen. He had a different plan. At its heart was uniting and galvanizing a workforce that possessed a deep and passionate pride for their blue oval, the iconic brand on every vehicle that drives out of a Ford assembly plant. What would happen if you could unite 250,000 employees – roughly the size of Ford's global operation – in a shared focus and effort?

Mulally knew that fundamentally the most important thing for success was to bring people together, to work with one another, to realize the vision and deliver the plan.[5] Mulally would soon prove that no matter how large the team is, inspired teamwork can be activated effectively and efficiently.

De-Activating Teamwork

History proves far too few people consistently unify a team's efforts effectively. Those who do win big. Mulally quickly saw the obstacles that were de-activating employee engagement and teamwork. Some of the more notable issues included:

1. The process for developing and recognizing leaders discouraged collaboration among team members. If anything, it encouraged isolation, positioning, and unhealthy rivalries.[6]

2. A hierarchical culture required employees to attain certain status or grade levels in order to communicate to those above them.[7] This restricted information flow and the relationships necessary for trust.

3. Fiefdoms, and loyalties to people rather than the company, required secrecy between functions and regions in several aspects of the business, including finances and production. Too often, alignment to one's boss took precedence over alignment to the customer and their needs.

4. Size meant complexity in processes and communication channels. Upon assessing the organization, Mulally stated, "There's no global company I know of that can succeed with the level of complexity we have at Ford."[8]

5. Fractured employee groups couldn't leverage Ford's unique automotive knowledge and assets. Not surprisingly, this meant innovation and new product development was flat.[9]

It Happens Everywhere

Intellectually, every person we've ever met understands the value of a team unified in a collaborative approach. Yet, human tendencies, outdated engagement techniques, and the influence of misaligned systems and cultural norms override the well-intentioned managers.

The de-activating circumstances Mulally encountered at Ford in no way are unique to Ford. To varying degrees these issues are present nearly everywhere. Yet everywhere, these conditions can be changed. What's necessary is the skill to activating inspired teamwork. And everyone can develop this capability.

Alan Mulally didn't change Ford – the employees of Ford changed Ford. Alan Mulally didn't build the cars customers wanted – the employees of Ford built those cars. What Alan Mulally did was rearrange employees' thinking, and this inspired them to act differently.

The greatness was always in the employees, waiting. Mulally's leadership was the instigator, the impetus that activated the greatness and generated the change.

It's Not How Smart You Are

For a moment, imagine you're an investor. You've got big money to put on the table, with the intention of gaining a return that will make you even wealthier. Your decision: You must choose the team that will outperform the competition in a game of various tasks, including decision making and problem solving. (This scenario actually happens every day.)

"Team Red" is composed of individuals whose average IQ is 118, about 18 points above the public average. "Team Blue" is composed of individuals who have ordinary, everyday IQ's, yet they have one individual on the team who has an IQ of 155. Which team would you bet on to win the competition?

With apologies due, this is a trick question. If Alan Mulally were reading this book with you, he'd likely tell you you're measuring the wrong success variable. Both teams may do well, because intelligence is a predictor of success. Yet, both teams will lose – and lose big – if they encounter a team in the market that has something else: the ability to work together.

If you bet on Team Red or Team Blue, you shouldn't be blamed. Countless organizations attempt to win in their market the same way: with a nearly singular focus on intelligence or talent *of the individual*. The thinking goes "the smarter and more capable individuals we have, the better we'll perform." So these organizations establish systems for attracting, hiring, training, and retaining *individuals*. Then they assess employee motivation and satisfaction, common measurements thought to be the best predictors of organizational success.

All the while, they miss the greatest predictor of a team's success. At some point, those smart individuals who are being hired and developed are going to bump into each other . . . and discover they actually have to work together to get something done.

What Predicts Your Team's Success

A group of people working together effectively is greater than the sum of their IQ's.[10] Researchers from Carnegie Mellon University, Union College, and MIT studied 699 people, teaming together in groups of two to five people, conducting exercises lasting up to five hours. Their assignment: Solve tasks including puzzles, those that required negotiating and brainstorming, and then expanded those tasks to architectural designs involving complex development problems.[11]

We manufactured the Team Red and Team Blue competition stated previously to represent what the researchers discovered: Average individual IQ and maximum IQ were poor predictors of group performance, while *collective intelligence* – the ability to work together effectively – was significantly stronger in foretelling group success.

The manner in which individuals interact matters. In fact, quality interactions are more important for success than the intelligence of each group member.[7] What determines the collective intelligence of a team? The researchers determined these three factors:

1. There was a significant correlation between collective intelligence and the average social sensitivity of the group members.

2. Groups where a few people dominated the conversation were less collectively intelligent than those with a more equal distribution of conversational turn-taking.

3. Collective intelligence was positively and significantly correlated with the proportion of females in the group.[12]

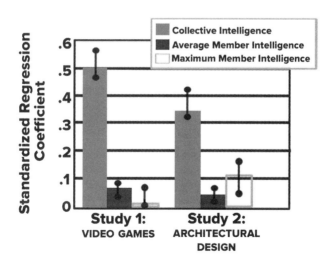

Regarding this last point: Men, don't lose hope. The experts make it clear that it's not necessarily the presence of women on the team that is the key factor to delivering a team's collective intelligence. It's social sensitivity, which is the predominant leading factor in collective intelligence, which is overly correlated to women. When Malone and the team controlled for the number of women in groups, it revealed that it was the emotional sensitivity effectiveness that won out. [13]

There are men who prove to be socially sensitive. Alan Mulally is the example featured here. And there are women who have proven not to be socially sensitive. We'll refrain from providing examples, though, as the point isn't a focus on gender; it's this: When you develop the capability within team members to be more socially sensitive and enable enhanced distribution of conversational turn-taking, your team will predictably perform stronger than your competition who may employ smarter people than you.

This is precisely what *ONE Team* delivers: a quick and effective method to facilitate these factors needed for greater success.

It's important to be clear: Emphasizing this collective intelligence study is not an argument against the development of the individual. Rather, this is an assertion that an equal focus and investment in how employees work together is woefully overlooked and essential for success.

Our experience informs us that it is the vast majority of organizations that claim "teamwork" as a value, yet undermine team effectiveness by elevating the focus on individuals. This means there is tremendous potential waiting to be activated within businesses.

Bottom line: Individual intelligence and talent counts, but teamwork rules.

Does Your Organization Foster A Climate For Inspired, High-Performance Teamwork?

Consider your organization and answer these true-or-false questions, then discuss your answers with your peers:

1. Our rewards system recognizes the cross-functional teamwork that delivers end-to-end for the customer.

2. The annual employee survey assesses for effective teamwork as thoroughly as it does for employee engagement and satisfaction.

3. We have a daily approach to building our culture (i.e., we leverage our interactions), rather than an "event-based" approach that where we talk about our work culture only during the holidays or when survey scores drop, etc.

4. We are assessed by our ability to effectively lead or contribute to teamwork as heavily as we are for our individual contributions.

5. Annual bonuses for team performance equal or exceed bonuses for individual performance.

6. We have "team performance reviews" as consistently as we have individual performance reviews.

7. There are no systems in place that pit teammates against one another, such as performance assessments that force a rating of a small group of individuals over others, reward and recognition programs that de-activate those who don't "win," information-sharing protocol, etc.

8. When we do acknowledge and celebrate individuals for reasons beyond the numbers they deliver, the nominating or voting is done by the entire team, rather than only the boss.

9. Customer information is shared seamlessly between people and functions.

10. When attending meetings, the majority of those with positional authority are effective at facilitating discussions among the team rather than spending most of the time talking at the team.

Results Never Lie

Ford is winning again. It has delivered profits every year since 2009 and its stock price has made a comeback. Mulally is considered among the greatest leaders of our time, overseeing one of the most remarkable corporate turnarounds in history.[3]

The changes in Ford's culture are all identified on the wallet-sized card Mulally provided every employee early in his tenure. In bold letters it reads "One Ford: One Team, One Plan, One Goal." The de-activating circumstances once present in the business gave way to systems and business practices that demanded transparency, alignment, collaboration, and trust – and inspired employees to own their responsibilities in the one-team culture.

Some may claim the causes for Mulally's and Ford's success were the financial decisions they made, including gaining financial support from banks prior to the 2008 economic collapse, a move Ford's competition didn't make, requiring them to accept government support. As well, the restructuring of labor contracts and agreements with Ford's unionized workforce also proved important. Or, others may argue it was Mulally's decision to eliminate brands such as Jaguar, Land Rover, and others that were financially draining and fragmenting the overall focus of the company.

These leadership decisions certainly are correlated to Ford's success. All are smart moves made by smart people. We do, though, submit that similar actions are taken by businesses everywhere on a regular basis: Organizations are constantly making adjustments in their financial approach, their product development, and portfolio. Why don't these organizations also achieve breathtaking growth?

Because they miss the additional, and even greater condition: Shaping and nurturing a culture where employees functions as one team. Ford didn't limit itself merely to smart people making smart decisions. Mulally transformed the way work got done by ensuring smart people worked together effectively. It was this act, in combination with other strategic maneuvers that elevated Ford's overall performance most significantly.

Alan Mulally was clear on this. He said "... at the heart of the One Ford plan is the phrase 'One Team.' Those are more than just words. We really expect our colleagues to model certain behaviors. People here really are committed to the enterprise and to each other. They are working for more than themselves."[14]

Amplify Your Input

What happens if you can't affect company policy or where people sit when they attend a meeting? How do you move a team forward when your influence is limited? The key is resisting the temptation to think that it's your power and wisdom alone that will do the job. The answer lies in using a mechanism, a tool, which amplifies your input and leverages the wisdom, knowledge, and experience of the whole.

While this act, this ability to activate inspired teamwork isn't difficult, history proves that remarkably few teams have individuals with the wisdom, skill, and courage to model what Alan Mulally and others have done.

A growing movement is changing that – and quickly.

Questions are levers. They activate, move and elevate thinking, which leads to different actions.

CHAPTER TWO:

How To Activate Inspired Teamwork

Move Your World

Archimedes of Syracuse, a Greek mathematician and physicist in the B.C. era, said, "Give me a lever long enough and a fulcrum on which to place it, and I shall move the world."[1]

Do you have a desire – better yet, do you have the ability – to move your world?

President Kennedy moved the world when he said, "Ask not what your country can do for you; ask what you can do for your country." Because it still echoes today, that planted question proved to have tremendous leverage. Kennedy had a fulcrum on which to place the question: a tremendous energy and passion for change. Consequently, Kennedy prompted and inspired us to think and act differently.

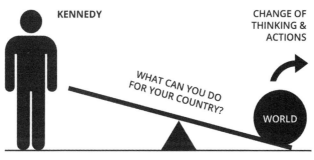

Questions are levers. They activate, move and elevate thinking, which leads to different actions.

Others have used the metaphor of questions as levers.[2] Most notably, it was Fran Peavey, in her superb work *Strategic Questioning*, who first explored the idea of a *long* lever question. She said, "Whenever we're doing strategic questioning, we're always looking for the motion." Long Lever Questions help people "go past the edge of what they know about themselves and discover new aspects."[3]

Peavey noted that some questions are more powerful, have more leverage, than others. "A good strategic question opens the options up. A long lever question opens up more possibility for motion than a short lever question."

Long Lever Questions are central to activating inspired teamwork.

Long Lever Questions

Based upon our years of experimenting and observing leaders highly skilled in asking questions, we're refining the description of Long Lever Questions to include any combination of the following qualities. The more criteria you satisfy, the greater success you'll have in strengthening any team.

LONG LEVER QUESTIONS:
1. Are forward focused
2. Drive inclusiveness and co-discovery
3. Elevate thinking, often connecting to purpose and desired long-term outcomes
4. Establish a specific focus on which the team can align
5. Accomplish full information flow
6. Are well-timed, therefore strengthen trust

It's also common for Long Lever Questions to:

1. Enable a team to efficiently and fully address issues that have been avoided
2. Inspire those around us, because they can generate possibilities

Do You Know This Person?

Bosses masquerading as leaders want to accomplish big things through improved teamwork but are using inadequate, short-lever questions (if they ask questions at all). A client we work with named Brady was such a person. (We've changed his name, but not his discovery.) Working for a global company, he'd worked his way up and was knocking on the door of a senior position. That's the moment his career stalled. He contacted us and in frustration reported that his team of scientists was performing well, "but I know in my bones they could achieve so much more." Brady's team had discovered the limits of their capacity for performance – but not their potential.

After observing his team in action we asked Brady to describe why he figured his team could do better. With little pause he provided a list of glaring behaviors that confirmed our perspectives:

1. For too long, achievement had improved only incrementally.
2. Cliques in relationships, based upon differing philosophies, were eating away trust.
3. Functions were finishing their work, and then throwing the product "over the wall" for another function to work on.
4. Individuals prioritized their own security and therefore were becoming increasingly risk-averse.
5. Several people were increasingly jockeying for status and recognition.
6. Information flow was anemic.
7. People lamented why others weren't motivated or were unwilling to be accountable.

Do you know any leaders like Brady? Based on more than 60,000 hours in observation of leaders and their teams in more than 30 companies located in 20 countries, we know that Brady is not alone in his experience. We've witnessed the symptoms Brady listed above and have seen their direct correlation to some team members' need to control or manipulate outcomes, dominate conversations, and use a preponderance of short-lever questions.

Our conservative estimate is that

the average leader is seldom asking questions at all, and when he or she does, over 90 percent of the questions have short levers.

To compound difficulties, the vast majority of those with the power of influence, when they do ask a question, seldom wait for answers or "overrule" responses by team members with their own opinion. Thus, the power of the question is negated.

Brady was no different: He's extremely well educated (holds a Ph.D.), has decades of experience, and is considered by some to be hyper when it comes to driving for results. It's also worth adding that he's an incredibly virtuous person; we consider him a tremendous friend. Yet, despite his good intentions, Brady ultimately realized *he* was imposing a limit on his team's performance. When we showed Brady his own Long Lever Question Feedback Form (sample in Appendix B), an assessment of how much he talks in meetings along with the types of questions he asks, he was first horrified – then embarrassed.

Even though Brady was always telling his team "I believe in you" and "I think we can achieve amazing things," his actions were a contradiction to that conviction. In meeting after meeting we observed him asking the same common short-lever questions we've seen hundreds of other leaders ask. We don't have a "top five most-asked leadership questions" list from our leader-shadow work, but if we did, it would look like Brady's:

Brady's Most-Asked Questions List
1. What do you think?
2. Are there any questions?
3. What's next?
4. What's the problem?
5. What are the results?
   Runner-up: What's the agenda for the meeting?

In the world of levers, these are toothpicks. They aren't *bad* questions. And to be clear, no one is suggesting their discontinued use. They have an important place in improving performance. Their prominence in the majority of workplaces, however, signals an important clue as to why so many teams fail to gel and consequently deliver mediocre levels of productivity. They're also a telltale sign as to why organizations are filled with people aching to find more fulfilling work.

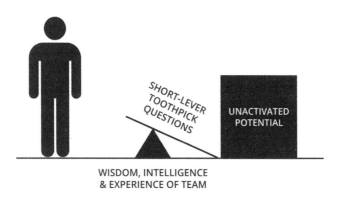

WISDOM, INTELLIGENCE
& EXPERIENCE OF TEAM

Toothpick questions fall far short in their ability to enable people to talk about what they want to talk about, indeed what they *must* discuss if they are to activate their one-team potential and influence improved performance.

A Boss Becomes A Leader

After a moment of contemplating the report in front of him, Brady said, "I tell my team I trust them. But my actions don't communicate that." His actions were about control, about his agenda, and he inadvertently disregarded the thoughts of those he needed to empower. With a new focus of activating the potential in his team through the use of Long Lever Questions, it didn't take long for Brady to move from "boss" to leader. Here's what some of his questions looked like. Compare his "top five" toothpick questions earlier with the types of Long Lever Questions Brady began to inject into his daily meetings:

1. In what specific way must we become more effective as a team that is also important to our customers?

2. What's the most important thing we need to achieve on this project so we know we're walking the talk when it comes to our quality objectives?

3. As you eye the future, where in our process development do we need to improve – and what difference will those improvements make?

4. When we're done with this effort, what's the experience we want to have as a team?

5. For us to have a breakthrough in this area, what would have to be true about our actions?

Upon a subsequent visit, as his team was eclipsing targeted objectives, one of those on Brady's team pulled us aside and said, "I don't know what you did to Brady. But keep doing it."

We didn't do anything to Brady. He did something for himself: He got better at activating the potential in others by asking Long Lever Questions.

Brady was fortunate. He had his moment of insight while his team was still functioning with an aspiration of improving their performance. The team still believed they had a potential they hadn't yet realized. This isn't always the case. In some situations we've been asked to support teams that first have to go through a recovery process. For too long they've been subject to bosses or other teammates who suppress and barrage them with short-lever – and often interrogative – questions:

1. Where are the results?
2. Did you finish?
3. Who's going to hold them accountable?
4. What part don't you understand?
5. Why are you behind?

Consequently, wedges had been driven between teammates, "silos" were reinforced, and me-first behaviors were necessary for survival. The idea of functioning as one team was so lofty that cynicism ruled.

Even these teams can recover, align, and become significantly more productive. "Cynicism," as American satirist Stephen Colbert said, "is a self-imposed blindness." Therefore, as a team develops the skill of asking Long Lever Questions, vision returns, they see greater things together, and the team comes back to where they once were: Realizing they do have potential and believing they *can*.

For resources to support your work with Long Lever Questions:
http://oneteambook.com/longleverquestions

Are You a Boss Or a Leader?

You know you're a boss when...

1. Others need you in order to get their work done.

2. You have to tell or remind people what level you're at in the organization.

3. People invite you to meetings because they have to (not because they want your ideas).

4. Employee salaries are seen as a "cost" rather than an investment.

5. "Climbing the ladder" is your top priority.

6. The best ideas are your ideas.

7. You get uncomfortable when you see lists like this one.

You know you're a leader who activates inspired teamwork when...

1. Those who respect you most often are those with whom you debate the most.

2. Productivity levels aren't determined by whether or not you're in the room.

3. Rather than only insisting on excellence, you facilitate the conditions for it to occur.

4. You're as interested in others' success as you are your own.

5. You hit your business growth targets *and* people want to join your team.

6. You know if you have a personnel issue, your leadership is also the issue.

7. No one knows where you park your car.

Words = Direction

What is your team talking about in meetings? Whatever it is, this much is certain: **What your team is talking about is where your team is going.**

Consider any meeting you regularly attend. During those meetings what percentage of time is spent talking about what the team *needs* to address in order to fulfill its purpose for gathering?

Not long ago, while preparing to work with a senior leader within a Fortune 100 organization, he shared how little value he was getting from the meetings that filled his calendar. "At best, we come out of meetings with common information. But what would happen if we exited a meeting with a common focus and language? A shared way of leading? Too often we're only exchanging data – and endlessly attempting to figure out why the results are so poor."

A team will *do* what it spends most of its time talking about. In order for a team to be successful tomorrow its conversations need to be different than they were yesterday. President Kennedy comprehended this. When discussing global conflict in his inaugural speech he said, "Let both sides explore the problems that unite us, instead of belaboring the problems that divide us." Kennedy knew that if the outcomes were to change, the conversations needed to change.

David Cooperrider, the father of the Appreciative Inquiry movement, along with author Diana Whitney and others, were the first to tell us that what your team is talking about is where they are going. Specifically, ". . . human systems grow toward what they persistently ask questions about."[4] Results never lie: The act of asking questions changes what a team is talking about and improves the results that team delivers.[4]

Yet, you might be as befuddled by this contradiction as we were: Despite the fact that organizations are filled with educated, intelligent, and experienced leaders who know that effectively crafted questions can drive greater change – the use of effective questions remains at alarmingly low levels. It is precisely that contradiction, as well as the realization of the tremendous potential locked within most teams, which inspired the research and effort behind *ONE Team*.

Un-Activated Teammates

Some managers claim they don't have time to ask bigger questions, so they rely on short-lever, transactional, task-completion questions that can often appear interrogative. A middle manager in a pharmaceutical company, when describing his boss, may have said it best: "When my supervisor asks me a question, he's not asking me to think. He's asking for an update on my progress . . . so he can save his skin."

Those using the "I-don't-have-enough-time" excuse (who, by the way, have the same amount of time as successful leaders: 24 -hours, to be precise) then spend exponentially more time suffering the consequences of a group of people who won't or can't unite as a focused team. Such teams are really groups of people who show up for work *un*activated. Left so too long and these same people are at risk of becoming *de*activated.

Any excuse for not asking Long Lever Questions is an insult to others.

If I told you, "I don't have enough time to learn and leverage what you think," what I'm really saying is, "I don't believe your ideas are as good as mine." Or worse, "I'm informing you that I don't think you're smart enough or good enough to do the job that needs to be done."

The real issue is that asking Long Lever Questions is a *skill*. Just like mastering a formula to eliminate waste or constraints in production is a capability to be learned, so is asking better leadership questions a skill to be developed.

As we increasingly observe teammates ask each other Long Lever Questions, research says something profoundly important begins to happen: Empathy is communicated. Rather than the low-value "how are you" type questions to which many cultures are numb, Long Lever Questions communicate the essentials of a trust community:

A. I believe in you.

B. Your ideas matter.

C. Our partnership in this effort is a priority.

As you increase your mastery of asking Long Lever Questions, you will become even more effective at diminishing the forces that suppress your team's performance. These forces have a specific cause, and more teams suffer from their ill effects than realized.

A **team** that achieves together tells the truth together. And they do it in a way that unites them.

CHAPTER THREE:

Use Your Power To Elevate Performance

Eliminate Your Team's Final Barrier

We call it the *High Performance Ceiling*. It's when a team has reached the limits of its performance capacity due to specific constraints in teamwork. Those restrictions are imposed when any team member demonstrates a behavior of power or control *over* others, thereby weakening teamwork. There is a direct correlation between the height of your team's High Performance Ceiling and your team's ability to function as one team.

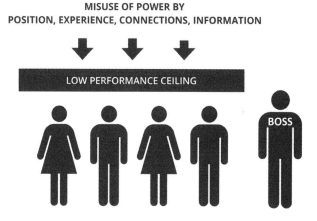

Every team we've seen suffers the limiting effects of this issue to some degree, either in subtle or overtly destructive forms. Even teams that perform at high levels are restricted in some way from their own version of this limiting behavior. In fact, from observing the leaders we respect the most, we know that if you're not continuously seeking methods for improving and elevating your High Performance Ceiling, you'll likely never sustain your current levels of excellence.

This is direct language, we know. That's the point: **A team that achieves together tells the truth together.** And they do it in a way that unites them. When a team discusses what needs to be talked about in their business, they can then take the productive actions to rise above and get past their High Performance Ceiling.[1]

Some people see their jobs as maintaining or guarding the ceiling. These aren't evil people; they simply have motivations that eclipse those of the team or believe they are somehow consistently smarter or better than those they see themselves grouped with.

Our belief, though, is

most people will readily and consistently devote themselves to inspired teamwork if they have the awareness and are equipped to do so.

Such was the case with the following executive.

"I've been selfish," Jim said. These aren't the words you'd typically hear from a VP in technology at one of the largest financial institutions in the world. But that's how Jim sees it. His team faces a pressure that can be measured in the millions of dollars. Should the technology his team is responsible for ever experience user errors, it costs big money. The team Jim is a part of is strong. Results never lie: Their work sets the standard in the industry.

High Performance Ceiling? The casual observer might think Jim's team doesn't have one. But Jim knows better, and he's determined to support his team in breaking through their ceiling. "I'm redefining my understanding of 'team.' I've been selfish in that I go into meetings and come to the team with a preconceived notion of what we need to do. My actions have been designed to get people to do certain things. This limits the team to the constraints of my thinking," Jim said.

With this new perspective, Jim could see the High Performance Ceiling he'd imposed on the team. "Everyone has different perspectives. If I can access those, I can activate our team beyond even the preconceived ideas I have."

When introduced to the idea of using Long Lever Questions to accomplish what he now wanted to get done, Jim said, "True confessions: Basically, all I ask are short-lever questions. And I think my favorite is 'What do you think?'"

Jim laughed and continued. "And when I ask that, what I'm really looking for is affirmation that what I'm thinking is right. Or it's code for 'Did you hear me?' and 'Are you going to do this?'

"I'm going to change my approach," Jim finished.

It may be obvious, yet it's worth stating: There's a correlation between

Jim's ability to tell the truth about his leadership and his team's ability to improve its performance.

Power Over People = Performance Barriers

Not elevating the High Performance Ceiling is costly. The power-over (rather than power-for) behaviors that form any team's upper limit can crush results. Consider this experiment conducted by Leigh Tost, Francesca Gino, and Richard Larrick (from the University of Michigan, Harvard University, and Duke University, respectively). Their work is exposing what leaders of high-performing organizations know: Teams that suffer poor or perpetually mediocre results are often led by people who have fallen prey to the deceiving idea that "a strong leader naturally improves the functioning of a team," writes Michael Blanding in his article about the study, *Pulpit Bullies: Why Dominating Leaders Kill Teams.*[2]

The key, of course, is how "strong leader" is defined. Power used for people is different than power over people.

Tost and the other researchers conducted several studies, all of which were equally convincing. In the most telling, teams were assembled for the purpose of advising a CEO on the best CFO candidate to hire. Leaders were appointed for each team. Some of these leaders experienced interventions reinforcing the idea "that each participant had unique insights to contribute. Other leaders experienced a much different intervention: They were primed to "feel powerful," meaning they were influenced to feel additional authority.

Which type of leader proved to be most effective? Blanding reports that groups with leaders who were reminded that their team could make contributions came up with the right answer an average of 60 percent of the time. Comparatively, "the (so-called) high-powered leaders who lacked intervention reminding them to listen to others" got the correct answer zero percent of the time.

It's worth repeating: The teams with leaders primed to feel additional authority scored a zero. They never succeeded. For teams that are subjected to such leaders who do not use their power wisely, the ceiling is so low people can't stand up, speak out, nor can they discover how great they can be.[3]

The solution for how to move past these limits lies in observing the dynamics the researchers observed in the successful teams. (We don't believe this will be a shock to many readers.) On the high-performing teams the (positional) leader was "stepping back," says Gino. "It's more of what you like to see, where the leader is orchestrating the conversation, but everyone is talking."

This is precisely what Long Lever Questions enable your team to do:

develop and foster the environment for everyone to effectively step up, speak out, and lead. Translated, when you ask Long Lever Questions you use your power for people to elevate the team's High Performance Ceiling.

You Have New Status: Step Up, Speak Out, And Lead

The era of "lean," the push to eliminate waste (including redundancies in job responsibilities), has elevated each employee to a new status: For any organization to sustain success every team member is expected to step up, speak out, and lead. Today, we are all responsible for demonstrating leadership behaviors once designated to the person sitting at the head of the table. Research allows us to predict that one-team effectiveness is only accomplished to the degree that each team member is accountable to this responsibility.[4]

But here's where it gets crazy. Managers aren't the only people who want the workforce to step up, speak out, and lead. Employees want the same thing! We still haven't met an employee anywhere who wakes up each morning and says, "I can't wait to be disengaged. HR is going to write new policies about me!"

Yet we've witnessed thousands of teams unable to accomplish what everyone wants: a fully and consistently energized team that functions with shared commitment.

Can you predict if a team will click in this way? Professor Alex Pentland and his team at MIT's Human Dynamics Laboratory set out to answer that question, and discovered a certain "buzz" in high-performing teams. Digging deeper, their research uncovered what every team needs to know and the wisdom they must implement if they are to realize their potential.

Establish A New Pattern Of Communication

Who talks the most on your team? Who talks the least? When do people step up and speak out? What sort of passion do they demonstrate? What's the tone in their voice? How frequently does the team meet face-to-face?

You don't have to verbalize your answers to these questions, but you are wise to consider them. Pentland's team found that more important than what your team is talking about is *how* they are communicating. The patterns of communication within a group are the most important predictors of a team's success.[5] In fact, patterns of communications "are as significant as all the other factors – individual intelligence, personality, skill, and the substance of discussions – combined," reported Pentland in an April 2012 *Harvard Business Review* article titled "The New Science of Building Great Teams."

These findings are consistent with the earlier study cited in Chapter One, of which Pentland contributed, that noted social sensitivity and equal distribution of conversational turn-taking as essential for a team's performance.

In this study, Pentland and his fellow researchers discovered the power of communication patterns in unique fashion. Working across a diverse set of industries, they found workplaces that had similar teams with varying performance. The teams included innovation teams, post-op wards in medical facilities, customer-facing teams in banks, backroom operations teams, call center teams and others. They then equipped employees with electronic badges that collected data regarding individual communication behavior. Tone of voice, body language, whom they had discussions with, how often and other data were collected.

With remarkable consistency, the data confirmed that the pattern of communication was paramount in team success. Summarized, the most effective patterns included these variables:

1. *The team communicates frequently.* In a typical project team, for example, a dozen or so communication exchanges per working hour may turn out to be optimum.

2. *Members of the team talk and listen in equal measure.* Lower performing teams have dominant members, teams within teams, and members who talk or listen but don't do both.

3. *The team engages in frequent informal communication.* The best teams spend roughly half their time having discussions outside formal meetings.

4. *Members explore for ideas and information outside the group.* High
performing teams periodically bring back to the team what
they've gained from outside sources.[6]

As part of their study, Pentland and his team deliberately rearranged
the communication patterns within teams. The results were quick to
be realized and impressive. In a bank call center, for example, average
handling time (the common measurement of effectiveness in such
operations) dropped by more than 20 percent among lower-performing
teams and decreased by 8 percent overall across the center. As well,
employee satisfaction increased by double-digits.[5]

How people communicate matters – in big ways.

Do You Believe?
Do you believe a one-team approach is essential to success? Those who do
demonstrate the belief in every move.

In May of 2013, A.G. Lafley returned to P&G as the CEO, nearly four
years after he had retired from the position. Seldom does anyone leave a
team, only to return to it. But P&G, the leading consumer packaged goods
company, well known both for its history of successes in the market as
well as its best-in-class approach to developing leaders, wasn't going back
in time. By rehiring Lafley they were, rather, accelerating the process
necessary to win with the consumer in the future: Leverage their size by
better coordinating their efforts.

In a letter to P&G employees, Lafley communicated his core beliefs.
Among the short list was this statement: "Every P&Ger is an owner and
a leader – we are one team, with one dream, collaborating internally and
competing externally."[7]

Each of us acts out of our beliefs, and Lafley is no different. Observations of the swift restructuring the global company is undergoing makes one thing abundantly clear: Every P&Ger's role and daily effort is now much more leveraged. Capitalizing on how resources are used – including how people work together – is the priority. Business functions are increasingly focused on specific industry and consumer groups. In short, Lafley is creating the conditions by which success can only be achieved through collaboration, focused sharing of resources and capabilities, and the development of trust and relationships among intra-company teams . . . that now must function as one team.

"I'm informing the team that we must redefine how we think of 'team,'" said a vice president within product supply. "It's incredibly invigorating to realize we're a part of something much bigger, and that our efforts now have a broader impact."

Rearranging an organizational chart, however, only clears a path for people to work together. It doesn't mean they will or can work together. This is how we've been supporting leaders across P&G: equipping team members with tools like Long Lever Questions to take advantage of the structure and systems they are in. The impact is immediate. "With the total leadership team cross-functionally equipped and committed to each other's success, we are unstoppable," one participant in a program said enthusiastically. "I have a great sense of 'one team, one dream.'"

History proves that a team with common objectives, shared truths, and which is equipped to act upon their values greatly expands the limits of their performance. The fact that this employee now believes what her CEO believes, and has a common language in the business approach, means organizational potential will more quickly become a reality.

Activate Inspired Teamwork

You may or may not have the authority to create a new organizational or team structure. No matter. To be frank, the source of our greatest inspiration comes from those who possess far less positional power, yet still step up and lead. Such people, deeply entrenched in day-to-day business, are the real change agents in the world. These are the individuals who, despite resistance from those who only know personal agendas, refuse to relent in their belief that together we are better – better at achieving and realizing the extraordinary vision. These are the people who walk into one meeting after another and demonstrate accountability to the team.

We see you, applaud you, and stand with you. Your determination to realize your potential by activating the potential of those around you proves to us that together we're closer to realizing greater achievements in all spaces of our society.

The 52 Activation Points that follow further enable you to quickly put your wisdom, and the research covered in this and preceding chapters, into action. As you move forward, something will happen: Your team will discover something profound and which the researchers can't quantify. That profound discovery is your one-team potential. When realized, you will achieve what you haven't before, and move yourself beyond what was originally thought possible.

Here's to activating greatness.

"Always the beautiful answer who asks a more beautiful question."

- e.e. cummings

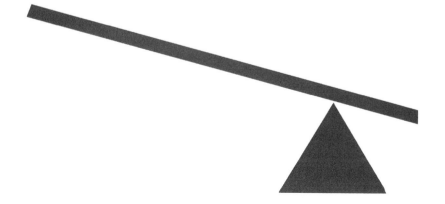

CHAPTER FOUR:

Developing One-Team Awareness

The Dangers Of Intellectual Sex

A certain word in the title of this Activation Point gets the attention of most. Unfortunately, so do a lot of other things. Without discipline of focus, teams have their attention pulled, splintered, and diverted from where it needs to be: executing plans and strategies.

This Activation Point is titled absurdly to support something high-performing teams know to be true: Too often teams are seduced into discussions that are intellectually stimulating – but ineffective from a productivity standpoint. Meetings meant to move performance forward turn into flights of cerebral calisthenics. (For the thinker in us it's oh so pleasurable.) But the result isn't what any of us want: a culture where little real work is done and success waits.

Over-planning, repetitive research (how much is necessary before you can act?), overanalyzing (including psychoanalysis of colleagues), reworking problems, overzealous risk assessments, regurgitations of experiences at the last company people worked for. . . like chocolate, we can't stop with just one comment. Ideas take days, even months, for team members to pontificate on, debate about, and talk over.

And the market yawns.

Are we talking about excellence or delivering it? Yes, "Imagination is more important than knowledge." (Thanks, Einstein.) But neither is worth anything if there's no action. Fulfillment is achieved through the action or expression of thought. This book and the discussions it inspires is not a substitute for execution. Each Activation Point is an exercise for strengthening a team's ability to transfer wisdom and knowledge into effective action.

What you think and talk about can only be measured by what you do. Realize your potential now: Act.

Long Lever Questions:

1. What type of, and how much, information do we need in order to make quality decisions?

2. In what ways can we improve our ability to move ideas into action quicker?

3. In daily interactions, what's our plan to use our growing awareness to transition conversations to more effective actions?

Are You "Nice" Or "Professional"?

As kids we were told, "If you can't say anything nice, don't say anything at all." The sage wisdom saved us from a few black eyes (and maybe a spanking).

The wisdom, applied as a professional in the workplace, however, stinks.

It's time to disobey our parents.

What are the essential differences between "being nice" and "being professional"? No team with aspirations of breaking through its high-performance block can succeed without collectively identifying where these two approaches diverge.

When we place more value on "being nice" than "being professional," tough issues, conversations, and topics are avoided. We delay or never provide the high-performance feedback that is accurate, sincere, and specific. And instead of avoiding the black eye from a teammate, the market gives us one.

The heart of this issue is respect. No professional wants to inflict pain on others. (It's not nice.) And because the truth can hurt, it's easy to avoid telling others how we *really* see a situation. When this happens, we squander an opportunity to increase performance and we inflict suffering on all.

A solution lies in evolving how we define and demonstrate respect. When respect means we act professionally to support others in delivering excellence, we are compelled to act quicker. Being a professional means we're no less empathetic. We care about other people's feelings and success. In fact, we care about those things so much that we *have* to tell our truth sooner rather than later. And, while that truth may be brutal, we don't tell it brutally.

Respect means embracing the responsibility of activating any potential that exists within ourselves and others in response to events, whether bad or good. "Being nice" creates a false sense of safety because it constructs a fragile network of counterproductive relationships. Professionals, however, know security lies not in their comfort, but in realizing potential.

One more thing: It's futile telling people, "Don't be so nice." You're fighting a lifetime of conditioning born from the imprinting of countless generations. (It's like telling people to be disrespectful of others. It isn't going to happen.) Equipping people to be more professional is the solution.

Long Lever Questions:

1. What are the important differences between "being nice" and "being professional" that are particularly relevant to our culture?

2. What's our vision for what it means to be a professional on this team? And how will we measure our ability to be more so?

3. What does it look like for us to tell the truth to each other *and* have each other's back?

This Is A Condition Of Your Employment

If I want to work for you, it's doubtful I can negotiate a lower standard for the company's definition of quality. And, if I disregard safety you'll probably send me out the door faster than I can argue my rationale for putting myself and others at risk.

But what about the people or team component of your culture? Can I show up with any mindset and behave or interact with others any way I choose and still work for you?

Many loudly declare that they "hire for attitude." Too often, though, something happens after the ink dries on the employment agreement. Perhaps these same people should emphasize that they "retain for attitude" as well; **organizations largely have a high tolerance for unproductive, team-sabotaging behaviors**. In these cases, the "people" aspect of culture is a lower priority than quality and safety – two areas where compliance is expected.

This isn't the reality everywhere, though. The leader at a large pharmaceutical plant in St. Louis, Missouri, inspires those who work with him by making it clear to them: "Quality work is a condition of our employment. So is safety. And how we show up at work, our mindset and how we treat others, is also a *condition of employment*."

This means that excellence in leadership and other behavioral competencies are on par with quality and safety as a priority. No surprise, his team consistently sets performance records.

Culture eats strategy for breakfast.[1] A team not able to demonstrate one-team behaviors can quickly make an exceptional business plan look average. Only teams that have employees who are both willing and equipped to model the values of all the elements of the company culture will fully activate the talent and potential around them. We deceive ourselves if we think anything less.

Long Lever Questions:

1. If people and healthy teams are strategic priorities, to what extent are we walking the talk?

2. What are the behavioral leadership and team competencies that are non-negotiable and critical to our business success?

3. What's our current plan to develop the behaviors that will differentiate us and provide our team with an edge in the market?

Is Your "Team Technology" Outdated?

I dare you: In your next meeting, tell your supervisor you want to use a computer operating system that worked quite well at a job you had in 1997.

Okay, so you know that will get you laughed at (or worse). This, however, provides the context: We can't interact with one another nor function as a team the way we did two decades ago and expect excellence today.

It's a common error in judgment that Marshall Goldsmith makes clear in his superb book *What Got You Here Won't Get You There*: The actions we took before created success; therefore, those actions always create success.

Any organization still using an outdated *human* operating system – the people component of any culture – that worked in a marketplace long ago can't expect a processing speed capable of keeping pace in today's world. The old operating systems are susceptible to viruses, glitches, user errors, and repeated breakdowns.

The top-down, non-inclusive, bureaucratic operating systems of yesterday were intended to create speed, but today result in non-responsive and slow-to-market processes. You can buy all the innovation apps you want, but the hard drive known as the culture will make the improvement efforts futile.

To compete you know you have to continuously improve your product. And you're investing in technologies to keep you relevant in the market. In terms of how your team operates together, are you benefitting from the same focus?

The market punishes those who attempt to deliver their goods on the back of outdated team dynamics and stagnant cultures.

The person next to you is different than she was in 1997. Is how you're functioning together, your team technology, keeping pace?

Long Lever Questions:

1. To what extent is our teamwork "modern" and strategically aligned with our current strategies?

2. What leadership approaches and cultural norms are we ready to shed? And why?

3. What sort of leadership style and teamwork components (i.e., values and principles) should we be developing to ensure we have sustained success in our market?

The Antidote To Communication Competition

"One team" means we're on the same team.

This seems obvious, yet too often we observe teams that forget. Consequently, they quickly slide into abysmal levels of productivity. The primary symptom or indicator that a team is at risk of such dysfunction manifests this way: Individuals have conversations for the purpose of winning them.

Conflicting priorities make for competing personnel. Even without clashing objectives, however, we all want to look good; we want to win. Yet, when some prioritize winning conversations over succeeding in our collective purpose, they greatly diminish the odds we'll win in the market.

One powerful antidote to communication competition is transparency. When all personal agendas are revealed (and we all have one), and we allow for full, free, two-way information flow, it's difficult to compete against one another. Use these questions to assess levels of transparency and communication competition:

1. When we debate ideas, what's our priority: proving others wrong . . . or mutually discovering the best path forward?

2. Does our tone and choice of words dismiss others as idiots . . . or are we activating the strength in the team by seeking diversity of thought?

3. Does our mantra of "the customer is first" require us to bludgeon each other with commands . . . or are our interactions as a team making us stronger as we go to market?

4. Do we fool ourselves by sending emails, thinking the electronic format provides a means for us to hide while firing missiles . . . or

do we seize moments of conflict to pick up the phone or walk down the hallway and demonstrate our professionalism?

The levels of transparency injected into communications predict what a team will accomplish. What is your priority as you enter into conversations? And do both parties share a common motive?

Long Lever Questions:

1. What does it look like for a team to become stronger as they communicate with one another?

2. In what ways can we become more transparent in our discussions? And how will doing so specifically impact our performance?

3. Who on our team can we learn from who regularly models transparency in communication?

What Your Customer Doesn't Care About

I like to think I care. But in this case, I didn't.

Halfway into a three-hour flight, the attendant informed the passengers, "Sorry folks. We no longer have water on this flight. We asked the ground crew several times to give us more, but they obviously didn't. So, this means no more drinking water, or coffee or teas. Or, for washing your hands. Again, I'm sorry about this, and we just have the ground crew to thank."

"Oh, good. I was worried it was your fault. I feel better now."

The fact that the flight attendant blamed our discomfort on someone else didn't make me feel better.

I don't care whose fault it is. As a customer my experience doesn't change because you've blamed someone else. My impression of your company, however, does.

In one breath the attendant gave us an insight into her corporate culture – and how she views teamwork. (It's safe to assume it's the point-your-finger and run-for-cover type). As well, we witnessed a person step away from a leadership opportunity; she said more about herself than the ground crew.

A high-performing team knows who they are, what they stand for, and what they're assembled to achieve. This identity informs the actions of

the individual. The customer only knows the label and promise of our brand. Is who we think we are consistent with how they see us? (Is who we think we are who we want to be?)

One team is a noble concept for a group of individuals on the inside of an organization. For the customer, one team is all that can be seen. As she decides whether or not to open her wallet, she ponders this question: Is this team capable of delivering the value they promise?

Long Lever Questions:

1. Whether our customer is internal or external, is that person's perspective of who we are consistent with the identity we have of ourselves?

2. How do we want to be perceived by our customer? And why?

3. As we deliver to our customer, what three specific ways can we function as one team even more consistently?

Bonus: What would you have done and communicated if you were the flight attendant above?

Why Are You Invited to Meetings?

We're teammates. I know what you can do. And you know what I can do. So is there any reason to have a meeting and expect something *better*?

A leader we serve is investing in discovering the "something" that can be taken from a meeting – that wasn't brought into it. "I want to accelerate our performance," she said, "by discovering what we can do *uniquely* together."

Your team is formed for the creation of delivering something that doesn't yet exist. (Does everyone know what that is?) It's the unique outcome only your team can do that can't be replicated by the competition. A one-team approach in meetings is a united, synergistic play at realizing something far greater than what one individual can accomplish. Inclusion is at the heart of inspired teamwork.

Those who attend meetings with a check-the-box or I-don't-want-to-be-here mindset splinter the team effort because they drive an exclusionary agenda. Unwittingly (or perhaps not), by isolating themselves they segregate others. This is toxic to a team.

As well, simply involving the multitude of talents, perspectives, and experiences that exist on a team isn't going to create the magic of one team. Just because someone is in a meeting doesn't mean he's included in the discussion.

Involving others is a step *toward* inclusion. Activating others *is* inclusion.

Inclusion occurs when we are dedicated to discovering a unique brilliance that can only be achieved together. Anyone not committed to the realization of this vision should not be long with the team.

Those committed to the one-team approach activate excellence in every interaction, regardless of who the other person is.

Accomplishing inclusion begins by including *ourselves,* by investing our inspiration and curiosity into the interactions we have with every person we meet. This activates others in ways that brings forth their investment of the same, resulting in an exponentially greater achievement.

Are you invited to meetings because you're smart? Or because you make those around you better?

Long Lever Questions:

1. We know the methods to create more productive meetings; where does the criterion of amplifying the greatness in others stand as a priority?

2. What can we do to more consistently discover what we can achieve uniquely together?

3. As our team engages other functions in the business, what do we want to model that reflects our team identity of inclusiveness?

Making Sure Families Get More Than "Leftovers"

You can see it down a long hallway: When people are struggling in their personal life . . . excellence in their professional life suffers. (We fool ourselves if we think we can hide it.)

Our parents' generation went to work and was expected to take off their "human-ness" like a coat and place it on a hanger. Then at the end of the day they retrieved their life, put it on, and resumed being themselves.

Those days are gone; work and life are integrated so thoroughly it's difficult to see or create the transitions between the two. And the fallout in failing in this shift is frightening: How much sense does it make to bleed, sweat, and toil at work . . . only to give your family your leftovers? ("Sorry, kids. I gave at the office.") Elite performance can't be sustained in companies that possess cultures where homes are turned into pit stops between days of endless racing.

You don't wait to be granted permission to pursue excellence at work. You don't need, therefore, an edict from above or a new company policy to empower you to live your values. As importantly, as a team, together you can model *life* excellence. Here's a powerful way to make that happen.

As teammates, the extent to which we have relationships with each other is the extent to which we'll work together.

The people at the table with you are not just individuals you need to work with to complete a task. They're mothers, fathers, children of aging parents, and community members; they've got a mortgage and fears and dreams. To recognize and honor another person's life (to communicate you care) is not to lower expectations for professional performance – it's a powerful way to elevate that individual.

We are a part of a larger community, filled with people who have dreams and pains similar to ours. It is in the consideration of the significance in the lives of those around us when we discover this: We are capable of doing more together because we're capable of *being* more together.

That teammate down the hallway, what does he need from you? Consider that as you answer, you ensure one more family in your community doesn't just get leftovers.

Long Lever Questions:

1. Is consideration of the whole-person approach important to us? And if so, why?

2. What does it look like for us to ensure high standards *and* consider the whole person next to us as we lead?

3. What can we do more of to create a culture that strengthens people – so they're even stronger in their family and community?

For videos and resources to support family, visit
http://oneteambook.com/family

The War For Problem Talent

Some people think they are fighting for success, but how they spend their time limits success.

The "war for talent" is real. You're not going to win in your market without the skill and capacity for excellence. This battle has three fronts: You need to acquire talent, develop it – and you'd better retain the talent you have.

Those in sales know it's more expensive to acquire new customers than it is to retain current clients. As it relates to talent, we can learn from this. And it starts with understanding where some managers are kicking their own butt.

Without knowing it, we can be seduced into participating in a war for *problem* talent. The "tyranny of the urgent" sucks the manager's focus to the problem aspects in the business. It doesn't take Sherlock Holmes to know that when we arrive at the scene we'll discover that it's often the problematic talent in the organization that's generating most of the difficulties.

In this moment our future is at risk. Because we go toward our focus, a consistent spotlight on problem talent submits us to a war or an effort to retain the wrong talent. Here's why: Top talent is left to fend for themselves as the problem talent consumes precious resources. This has a splintering effect within the body whole.

Where are you spending your time:

1. With the employee who didn't deliver expected results – or the one who's pleasing customers most effectively?

2. Talking about the manager who peeves his peers – or the one who collaborates effectively?

3. Discussing individuals who generate chaos – or those who lead forward with clarity?

While addressing employees who are making things difficult is essential, top talent deserves and warrants a focus that inspires and compels them to stay.

Long Lever Questions:

1. As it relates to supporting top talent, what do our actions and use of resources communicate to the organization?

2. Regarding our top talent, what focus and daily actions will most accelerate their performance?

3. As a team, why is this transparency on how we attract, retain, and activate talent important?

The Most Important Decision Of A Career

When you started your career all you knew was success. You moved quickly. People talked about you. Potential was high; you could see yourself in roles beyond the traditional. It all seemed easy.

With success came new responsibilities. You learned at voracious rates. As you did, grander experiences delivered ever-expanding expectations. Then something slowly changed. Somewhere, somehow, things began to get cluttered. Expectations weren't met. The simplicity faded; opportunities became gray.

Until you found yourself here, at perhaps the most important decision you'll make in your career. What will you believe about yourself? Perhaps you weren't as good as you thought. Or maybe there's a conspiracy of forces unseen that, no matter how hard you push, keep you in the same spot. Day after day.

Possibly, though, there's another explanation. Life hasn't changed. There remain as many (if not more) opportunities as before. What's changed is the focus on a particular type of learning. Where once you thought "How do I?" it somehow slipped to "Darn, why did I?" And if this misguided focus is the reason for inspiration lost, then this guided center of attention allows you to reclaim what you truly want to experience: growth.

By the way: Those who no longer invest the energy in stretching themselves will attempt to persuade you to succumb to their misery. "It's no use," they'll chide. Your success is a reminder of their failure.

Tip your hat to them, and carry on. By doing so you will attract to your team a band of like-minded, lifelong achievers, eager to find out how far you can go together.

Long Lever Questions:

1. On a scale of 1 to 5 (5 = Strongest), how would you rate our team as "a band of like-minded achievers" committed to and passionate about learning? What's the rationale for your score?

2. Continuous improvement is the step beyond continuous learning; therefore, how do we know we're learning what we can and should be in our work?

3. What elements of our team culture can we develop even more to ensure we're increasingly making it safer for teammates to learn as they work?

You Can't Buy This – But Need It

Your team can buy a lot of things it needs to be a success. Talent, faster machines, smart consultants, and full-page ads in the Times. "But what you can't buy," a leader told me, "is history."

Legacy qualities, such as situational knowledge, emotional connections, "got your back" loyalty, and an ownership mindset, all these and more come by honoring and leveraging the unique past each established company possesses.

These days it seems that start-up companies have the advantage. In a crazy-fast world, they're more nimble, and several are flush with cash. Crazy as it sounds, we see some of their competitors, organizations with decades of experience, willingly chuck aside one of their few competitive advantages: their legacy attributes. Often, this is not deliberate. They just don't know what they don't know.

Where we need to go can stand in stark contrast to where we currently stand – and that means where we are is "bad." Downright scary in fact. Which, by default, means everything we did to get where we are now (and everyone who did it) was wrong.

"We never" and "they always" become (un)intended allegations and indictments that our history has not served us well. In extreme cases, corporate history and the people associated with it are demonized.

The cost is severe when we blame our past for who we are now.

We forfeit a resource no one else has. It's true: What got us here won't get us there.[2] But what got us here is a period in time filled with remarkable people, tremendous successes, extraordinary lessons, and an identity of perseverance. These assets have the potential for informing and influencing the future in nearly limitless ways.

That is a resource you cannot buy.

Long Lever Questions:

1. When we speak about our team and company, to what extent are we communicating an acceptance and appreciation for past efforts?

2. Where's the line between honoring the past and effectively leading change with urgency and efficiency? How do we effectively do this?

3. What got us here won't get us there – yet, what is it that got us here that can prove to be a resource for getting us to where we want to go?

Big Ideas That Provide The Fulcrum Of Wisdom For Your Long Lever Questions

Activation Point: Execution

Without discipline of focus, teams have their attention diverted from where it needs to be: executing plans and strategies. Are we talking about excellence or delivering it? What you think and talk about can only be measured by what you do. Realize your potential now: Act.

Activation Point: Honesty

There are essential differences between "being nice" and "being professional." The heart of this issue is respect. A solution lies in evolving how we define and demonstrate respect. Respect means I embrace the responsibility of activating any potential that exists in myself and others in response to events, whether bad or good. And, while telling the truth may be brutal, I don't tell it brutally.

Activation Point: Culture

"Quality work is a condition of our employment. So is safety. And how we show up at work, our mindset and how we treat others, is also a *condition of employment*." Culture eats strategy for breakfast. Only teams that have employees who are both willing and equipped to model the values of all the elements of the company culture will fully activate the talent and potential around them.

Activation Point: Teamwork

We can't interact with one another nor function as a team the way we did two decades ago and expect excellence today. To compete you have to continuously improve your product. The market punishes those who attempt to deliver their goods on the back of outdated team dynamics and stagnant cultures.

Activation Point: Transparency

When some prioritize winning conversations over succeeding in our collective purpose, they greatly diminish the odds we'll win in the market. One powerful antidote to communication competition is transparency. When all personal agendas are revealed (and we all have one), and we allow for full, free, two-way information flow, it's difficult to compete against one another.

Activation Point: Identity

A high-performing team knows who they are, what they stand for, and what they're assembled to achieve. This identity shapes the actions of the individual. The customer only knows the label and promise of our brand. Is who we think we are consistent with how they see us? (Is who we think we are who we want to be?)

Activation Point: Inclusion

A one-team approach in meetings is a united, synergistic play at realizing something far greater than one individual can accomplish. Inclusion is at the heart of inspired teamwork. Involving others is a step toward inclusion. *Activating* others is inclusion. Accomplishing inclusion begins by investing our inspiration and curiosity into the interactions we have with every person we meet.

Activation Point: Empathy

Today, work and life are integrated so thoroughly it's difficult to see or create the transitions between the two. As teammates, it is in the consideration of the significance in the *lives* of those around us when we discover this: We are capable of doing more together because we're capable of *being* more together.

Activation Point: Talent

Without awareness, a consistent spotlight on problems in the business means a constant focus on problem talent. Then, top talent is left to fend for themselves. This has a splintering effect within the body whole. Who we spend our time with is key.

Activation Point: Learn

A guided focus on learning allows us to claim what we all want to experience: growth. By investing energy in stretching ourselves, we attract to the team a band of like-minded, lifelong achievers, eager to find out how far we can go together.

Activation Point: Legacy

The cost is severe when we blame our past for who we are now: We forfeit a resource no one else has. Legacy qualities, such as situational knowledge, emotional connections, "got your back" loyalty, and an ownership mindset, are a resource you cannot buy.

Download a quick reference of all chapter summaries at
http://oneteambook.com/chaptersummaries

Where are we in our development of activating an inspired, one-team approach?

These questions further elevate the High Performance Ceiling by activating the potential you've created while working through Activation Points I through II. We encourage you to record your answers for reflection and comparison to future assessments. Both consistencies and contrasts will mark your development as one, inspired team.

A. *As we answered the Long Lever Questions, what did we discover about ourselves that's important to our work together moving forward?*

B. In the introduction of this book, there were two questions we had to ask ourselves, one of which read: Why is it important to each of us that we develop inspired teamwork? *In what ways are we beginning to see that motivation realized?*

C. *What can we do more of as we move through future Activation Points to deliver on this motivation?*

D. *Which Activation Point in Chapter Four was particularly important to our development as a team? Why?*

Successes from the Field

Long Lever Questions In Action

Delivering Quality Around the Clock

What were you doing at 2 a.m.? It's likely you were sleeping like we were. But this next leader wasn't. Instead, he was discovering how exceptional his team really is.

What's necessary for your team to deliver extraordinary results regardless of the hour? Your answer reveals something powerful: your philosophy of leadership and teamwork.

"It's about inspiring people to be better – and a 'better' that is defined by them," said Jeff, a leader within information technology (IT) at one of the world's largest financial services organizations. Jeff's understanding and use of Long Lever Questions has propelled his team to exceptional performance.

In order to ensure quality service is uninterrupted to online customers, the IT department at most online banks "releases" new software implementation while you and I are sleeping. The stakes are high and intense: Each release must be completed within a short window of time and with precision that delights the customer. And while it may appear to happen overnight, the preparations are extensive.

"It required 250,000 effort hours to accomplish this release," Jeff said. While many would wait until the midnight hour to give a famous speech, that's not Jeff's method. Weeks prior to the release, had you shadowed him on the job, you would have found Jeff asking very specific Long Lever Questions that mirrored his philosophy on leadership and teamwork – and built the foundation for success.

What were some of the most influential Long Lever Questions he asked?

"At a town hall meeting I emphasized to everyone that our primary goal was to always improve, always get better. We are so used to showing up to work and staring at PowerPoint decks and tons of information that it's easy to get detached from it all. I'm not surprised people default to just going through the motions. Yet, I believe if you're going to succeed, you have to make this work personal. So, I asked those present to write on a piece of paper their answer to this question: What does 'better' mean to you – and at the end of the day, what are you doing to get better?"

Jeff explained, **"If you can't answer that question then you need to change what you're doing."**

What makes Jeff unique – and powerful in his influence – is his actions communicate an untarnished belief that people will be great if you give them the opportunity. It's easy to imagine the ordinary manager wanting to check the answers written by subordinates to ensure the answers are "correct." For Jeff, the correct answer is the one that inspires greater, more productive actions. Therefore, there's no need for Jeff to check answers.

On another occasion prior to the release, Jeff informed his direct reports that if they wanted to see changes in the culture, they had to model even more the behaviors they wanted to see. Next came the Long Lever Question: "What are three attributes you want to model that will drive your definition of success?"

"What's fascinating," Jeff said, "is these Long Lever Questions create and open a dialogue that hadn't existed before. People might have been thinking the thoughts I asked them, but they weren't saying them." And certainly not in the context of the team.

Results never lie. Jeff and his team delivered in exceptional ways. "The release speaks for itself," Jeff said. "At the conclusion of the release our defect rate came in at less than one-half of 1 percent." To put that into perspective, for a similar release and team size, the industry average is 75 to 100 defects. Jeff's team only had 9.

It's estimated that such a low defect rate – or successful release – will save a company like Jeff's $5 million to $15 million. "But what's amazing to me," Jeff said, "is I truly believe this team hasn't reached their potential. I know we're going to do even greater things."

Jeff's ability to elevate the quality of his leadership by asking Long Lever Questions is directly correlated to the quality his team delivers – especially when it matters most.

Developing The Skill Of Using Long Lever Questions

The Prize Comes *After* The Question

It's a sight like no other: When young children at a party open gifts, the thrill of discovery is electrifying. What's underneath the wrapping paper? What's in the box? The moment of unwrapping presents brings everyone to attention.

Adults are no different, and well-crafted questions have a similar effect.

This is, though, a cautionary note to those who want to use the power of their influence *for* the team rather than *over* the team. In the thousands of hours spent observing how questions are asked by well-intentioned team members with varying types of power, we've witness three destructive behaviors after the question is stated:

1. *They ask, and then quickly answer the question themselves.* Comfort in silence, security in allowing others to process and think, is a must for questions to be effective in elevating performance.

2. *They ask, and then move to another topic with barely a pause.* This unwittingly informs the team that the questions they ask are "rhetorical" and ultimately trains others to stay quiet. If a question is asked, allow it to work.

3. *When others on the team do answer, the "leader" (positional or otherwise) then closes the conversation by weighing in with his or her thoughts.* These leaders are at risk of subtly informing team members their answers are wrong. Additionally, if there are quiet members on the team, they know if they stay quiet long enough, the boss will ultimately tell them what the "correct" answer is.

A question is only as strong as the subsequent actions it prompts.

Imagine bringing a wrapped gift to a party, and then denying another the opportunity to open it. Or worse, claiming the prize by opening the wrapped present yourself in front of everyone else.

Few people would do such a thing, yet we see well-intentioned leaders commonly commit the three errors listed earlier when asking questions. The best questions are like a wrapped gift. The prize lies after the question mark. It behooves inquirers to flex their awareness and mind their actions after they've asked their question.

What To Do If They Won't Answer The Question

Patricia was serious about activating the potential within her team. After being equipped and trained with leadership tools, including Long Lever Questions, she was in a hurry to apply what she learned.

To support Patricia's team in sustaining and growing their new skills, we met with them after several weeks had passed. This is when a somewhat aggravated Patricia approached us and said, "I love the idea of asking Long Lever Questions, but I can't get anyone to answer them!"

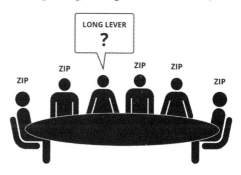

It was certainly easy to empathize with Patricia. Many workplaces have conditioned people to be intellectually lazy. Responding to questions that require people to think can be tremendously uncomfortable or even threatening to some.

We side with leaders, however, who think failing as a team is much more uncomfortable or threatening than asking and answering questions.

As an activator of improved performance, you are not on the team for the comfort of others. You are where you are to fulfill potential.

Patricia has a courage shaped by a determination to experience and deliver excellence. With rigor, she embraced these five techniques, all of which have proven effective at ensuring questions deliver improved responses and outcomes:

1. Embrace the wisdom that silence can be the sound of productivity. Our go-faster world has created the illusion that if people aren't moving or talking then they're not being productive. This is far from the truth. Overwhelmingly, our surveys show that people rarely have time to "reflect" while working – and yet when they do, they're more productive.

2. When extended silence is experienced, let this "gift" sit. Consider the silence in the room or on the phone as your statement to the team: "I believe in your wisdom so strongly that I refuse to do the work for you." Eventually someone will respond – or a team member will ask you to restate the question. And, by being happy to do so, you'll advance the thinking on the team.

3. For teams that are exceptionally quiet, or on conference calls where it's easy for people to "hide," its proven effective to periodically have people write their answers to questions. This takes a moment of silence, yet the outcome is impressive: When people write their thoughts down, it activates parts of the brain that are otherwise not used. Additionally, once you've asked people to write their answers, you can now call on anyone you'd like to hear from. You've respectfully given them the opportunity to consider their own ideas prior to having them share publicly.

4. If you know the question you're going to ask in an upcoming meeting, it's helpful to share that question in the meeting notice or invite, along with the note "I'd like to hear answers from several of you." This provides your team members an opportunity to consider their responses prior to the meeting.

5. If you have a team where certain people dominate conversations, periodically break the team into groups of two or three and have people share their answers in their clusters. Now, on a team of 10 people, instead of only one person speaking and dominating the focus, you have several people talking, which means:

   a. You've significantly improved the odds that you'll activate diverse responses.

   b. Everyone participates, rather than just the verbose few.

   c. The introverted individuals on the team now have a "safer" environment to experiment with and express their ideas.

Unquestionably, the above techniques are unconventional. This is precisely the point: It's the progressive teams who consistently realize the prize by raising their High Performance Ceiling.

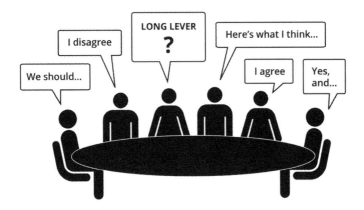

Patricia and others who have pioneered techniques such as these with their team report that they initially receive raised eyebrows and "what are you doing?" looks. Yet, as Patricia said, she can't expect her team to innovate and deliver improved performance if she doesn't first innovate her leadership techniques.

Which Makes You Most Nervous?
Which causes you more anxiety: the team you're on won't elevate their performance, or the team you're on will eye you suspiciously for doing something that's not "normal"?

We intend to see the day when Long Lever Questions are increasingly "normal" in every organization serious about continuously improving their performance.

To assist with any anxiety you may have about asking Long Lever Questions, we encourage you to use a platform statement or a message that informs the team why you are asking them these questions. As an example, you could say, "I'm going to change my approach a bit in terms of how I contribute to this team because I want us to stretch and be challenged. I know we have a greater potential that can be activated."

The Value Of Confusion

In addition to silence in response to questions, many of us have experienced asking a question, only to hear a response that doesn't come close to answering the question. "When this occurs, I have been quick to discredit the other person as being confused," a friend told us. "With closer thought, though, I realize that the person is providing valuable information to me. He's telling me what he's struggling with, perhaps his pain point or his biggest challenge.

"So while I may not get to go where I wanted to with my question," she added, "I get a sign of what needs to be addressed before my question can be answered."

The confusion of others is so consistently dismissed or criticized in some organizations that people learn not to confess their misunderstandings. This means that as these people walk away from the meeting, with each step they extend their confusion deeper into the business.

Expressed confusion provides value because it shortens the distance to clarity.

Looking for additional strategies to support
productive, efficient, and effective meetings? Visit
http://oneteambook.com/meetings

CHAPTER FIVE:

Creating
One-Team
Alignment

The Mindset For High Performance

"If they knew what our world looked like they would understand why we're not successful."

Don't believe the malarkey. We live in the same world, with similar conditions creating nearly identical pressures. Authors Jim Collins and Morten Hansen[1] report that top performers are no luckier than the average achiever. They don't have different circumstances – they have different behaviors.

Let's take a closer look at the elements necessary for high performance. As you review the list, consider your reaction to these events:

1. Mistakes

2. Conflict

3. Lack of resources

4. A customer saying, "No thank you."

Teams destined for mediocrity are seduced into thinking the above situations only happen to mediocre teams. They experience these situations and then point fingers and throw their hands up, relinquishing their ability to discover the magnitude of the opportunities in front of them.

Everyone knows the list above; we're all being tested. High-performing teams galvanize themselves with a mindset that filters these circumstances, spending less time in frustration and more in inspiration:

Mistakes . . . are accepted and seen not as trial and error, but trial and *learn.*

Conflict . . . is welcome, as team members may debate an idea, but not fight with each other.

Lack of resources . . . is an excuse that has no merit; the "dilemma" is the genesis of innovation.

A customer saying, "No thank you" . . . inspires us to question our biases and listen for clues to growth.

There is a myth that high-performing teams never lose, everyone on the team likes each other, and team members have a lot of extra time and resources. In reality though, they're just like you.

Long Lever Questions:

1. To what extent and in what important ways do we have the mindset for high performance?

2. How do we get better at modeling a high-performance response to the challenges we face?

3. What challenge are we currently facing where we can better apply our mindset for high performance?

If You Have This Instinct, Trust It

They want you to think your idea for innovation won't work. They'll tell you there is a lot of evidence to prove it won't. As well, reasons for failure surround you: the bureaucracy, the politics, other departments throwing banana peels in your path, the irrational market – it's enough to convince you that your goal is impossible.

Scoff at such notions. Trust your instincts.

Teams that realize their potential have an impulse for excellence. The reality of their circumstances is no different than that of their competitors; they just experience the circumstances differently. As leaders, they suspend the conundrum; they silence the echoes of fear; they trust the notion of possibility. They move quickly to answering these types of Long Lever Questions:

1. Given the circumstances, what is the best we could ever do?

2. What has to be true for success to happen?

3. What exists that gives us the confidence we can succeed?

4. What strengths do we possess that enable us to persevere?

5. In what ways have we proven ourselves resilient, agile, and capable in similar situations?

Loudly reject the claims of the cynics. They speak a language based in fear, designed to intimidate and blur your vision.

They want to release themselves from future responsibility, from the fear that they may not be perfect.

Excellence isn't found in generating the perfect idea or solution, but in using your wisdom to deliver – and move to more doors of discovery and possibility. When your instincts give you courage and inspiration, trust them.

Long Lever Questions:

1. With what project are we ready to ask the Long Lever Questions listed earlier in this Activation Point – and why?

2. What does it look like for us to effectively suspend a current reality and invite additional perspectives?

3. What are the instincts of excellence our team possesses?

Why Wimps Shouldn't Be Blamed For Not Speaking Out

"We're avoiding the tough issues," the manager said. "If we had more courage to talk about what needs to be said, we could move forward much faster."

On the surface it looks like the easy solution: Have the guts to step up and speak out and make the tough decision. But perhaps those claiming others are wimps should reconsider. If we ask this same manager to walk into a burning house or step in front of a firing squad we likely would see a similar deficit in courage.

Some cultures don't support team members who choose to be courageous by stepping up and speaking their mind. In a culture of judgment, where the court of opinion delivers severe consequences, who wants to commit career suicide by saying the wrong thing? It can seem easier to stay quiet.

True, more courage modeled by everyone would make for a stronger team. Focusing on and blaming the "wimps," however, makes more wimps. The breakthrough possibility lies in having the courage to develop an environment that's safe for others to step up and speak out earlier than they normally would. Teams that activate one-team performance do this by:

A. Equipping themselves to model values that actuate and reward diversity of thought.

B. Being as interested in the success of their peers as they are in their own.

C. Developing stronger relationships each time they interact with one another.

When we "have each other's back" it's not courage we have to summon; rather, it's the greatness in others we're eager to reveal. The audacity in making this shift means we can shock even the market.

Long Lever Questions:

1. The dynamics outlined in A, B, and C can't be faked. Where are we already strong in these areas?

2. What opportunities do we have to demonstrate that we "have each other's back" – and what differences will that make?

3. Because we can say what needs to be said, what issue or topic should we demonstrate more courage with and discuss now?

Mr. Fix-It And His Fatal Mistake

You can make a living fixing or averting problems. Root-cause analysis, failure analysis, risk management, cost containment – master these and you'll be in demand. There'll always be margins to preserve, costs to eliminate, a customer to save, processes to repair, and systems to patch.

But your leadership won't be coveted. Repairing damage done in the past or avoiding it tomorrow doesn't mean you're capable of influencing the future by developing people and teams to think and act differently.

Fixing problems, putting out fires, isn't leadership. They are acts of control management. They don't build capacity in the system. Influencing greater growth, accelerating the development of capability – creating the future – that's leadership.

The distinction between fixing something and developing someone is significant. When misunderstood, the well-intentioned question "What's the problem?" can doom a team to dysfunction: What starts as a quest to learn what went wrong (so we can fix the problem) suddenly spirals out of control as teammates respond with finger pointing and other defensive postures. Consequently, capacity and productivity collapses.

Whether we like it or not, emotions rule over logic and reason. The fatal mistake occurs when Mr. Fix-it forgets he's leading people rather than the machines or spreadsheets he's mastered. Then, instead of fixing problems, his leadership (or lack of it) becomes the problem.

Effective teams neutralize the technical, the task, or the issue.

Rather than asking about the problem (and therefore risking unhealthy conflict), they create the conditions for a rapid shift in focus to solutions by inquiring, "What's the issue? What data do we have? What perspective should we consider? What do we need to know in order to move this forward?" This approach, as author Liz Wiseman says, has a "multiplying" effect, as potential and capacity in the workforce increases.[2]

Teams that move beyond their High Performance Ceiling have deeper, more meaningful discussions about real issues not because the people were once broken and are now fixed; rather, they developed the ability to more effectively talk about the problems they face.

Long Lever Questions:

1. What would have to happen in our cultural approach to ensure we get stronger as a team each time we face a "problem"?

2. Currently, when we address issues (a.k.a. problems), to what extent are we developing people and partnerships with each other in the process?

3. What does it look like for us to be even more honest with each other and address "real" issues – and grow stronger as a team in the process?

The World's (un)Luckiest Employee

I met the world's luckiest employee. Actually, I didn't meet him: I met his boss.

I was alone in the hotel gym when the door opened. A man with a tie entered, and I watched as he looked around and then pressed a button on his radio. "Mike," he said after the beep. "I'm down here in the gym. We need the towels picked up. More fruit at the stand. And the water is nearly empty."

"Okay," came the crackled response.

Wow. Imagine never having to think while you work. Mike may well be the world's luckiest employee! He has a manager who processes everything for him.

Just show up on time and plug me in, Boss.

If Mike wants something more from his life and career, however, if he wants to realize who he's capable of being, he is the world's *unluckiest* employee. With a boss like "radio man" he's confined to the limits of his supervisor's sight. And the hotel's growth is doomed to the restrictions of how fast the radio man can make his rounds.

How lucky are your employees?

1. Because of the correlation between individual contributions and our ability to meet our growth objectives as a team, in what areas of our business can we give more responsibility to others?

2. What does it look like in our day-to-day operations to fully trust others to drive our business forward? Where can we do more of this?

3. What's the link between developing capacity in others – and the level of fulfillment they experience in their work with us?

When Playing It Safe Hurts

To survive as humans we are programmed to protect ourselves. Reduce risk. Think. Assess. Think again. Prevent death from unnatural causes.

Today's market, however, is turning a trick: Wait or play it too safe and you *don't* survive.

Health and safety within organizations are a non-negotiable. There is another "safety" issue, however, that must be addressed if teams are to succeed: when a team member chooses to "play it safe" by not saying what needs to be said or doing what needs to be done. This sort of safety lowers the High Performance Ceiling by reducing the ability to activate and realize our greater potential.

"Playing it safe" as a team member takes many forms:

1. Saving a reputation – rather than being honest about data. It's unsafe for the "ego" to tell the truth about what we see. *Establish a new safety benchmark by praising truth-telling. When "bad news" is shared in a manner that activates problem solving, make the messenger of such a hero.*

2. Intentionally undervaluing the contribution we can make – thereby ensuring we hit our targets. *Reward those who model transparency of numbers and their potential, so rather than seeing how safe we can be, we discover how great we can be.*

3. Keeping our mouth shut – because offering an alternative perspective means we could be wrong (gasp!). It used to be irresponsible to say the unthinkable; now it's irresponsible not to. *When you hear diverse ideas, express enthusiasm for the conflict in perspectives.*

4. Only praise and reward those who regularly achieve their objectives – and banish those who took risks and failed. **Deliver acclaim and reward those who may not win today, but who discover what is necessary for victory tomorrow.**

Sincere but misguided approaches, feedback, and systems destroy risk taking and innovation. The consequence for not transforming these dynamics is that you won't know who you are or who you can become. And if you don't know that, how can you expect the customer to know the same?

Long Lever Questions:

1. In what ways might we be playing it safe – and how is that leaving potential unrealized?

2. Where and how can we enhance our feedback and rewards for those who take risks and fail, yet prepare us for victory tomorrow?

3. What actions must we model to make it safer for those around us to step up and speak out?

I Blowed It Up

"You mean you *blew* it up," I explained to my 5-year-old who a moment earlier had been holding a balloon. She looked at me like I was a fence post. "No, Dad. I blowed it up."

My wife interjected, "Honey, if we don't use words properly, people won't know what we're saying."

Now our daughter was looking at two posts. "If I know what I'm saying how come other people won't know what I'm saying?" she said.

We speak from pictures we see clearly in our head, and often assume others see the same image. The vision of what we believe the team must achieve is as clear to us as a still-life painting by Monet. The path through the garden (what success looks like) is so vivid we could jump into the painting.

But what do others see when we speak? If we're not careful, they see a Kandinsky painting: Everything is in the abstract.

1. They say, "We must deliver excellence!" We wonder, "What does excellence look like?"

2. They declare, "Quality is an imperative!" He walks away asking, "What constitutes quality?"

3. They insist, "The customer is our top priority." She questions, "But where do they stand among my other top priorities?"

Discussions rich with questions create a language of excellence. These are effective alignment questions that make that which we want to see in the future clear for both team members:

1. What does success look like to you?

2. How will you measure progress?

3. How will you restate these objectives from your perspective?

4. What do you feel are the most important action steps today?

5. What standard will you use to assess your work?

For a team to have vision, it means we must see the same thing. If we don't incorporate such questions into our discussions, there's little wonder why we might blowed it up.

Long Lever Questions:

1. What questions can we ask to ensure better alignment during our daily conversations?

2. With what projects do we know we "see" the same picture of success? And what did we do to establish such alignment?

3. What's our plan to be more accountable to asking alignment-of-vision questions in meetings?

Free Gas For Life

Running on empty. That's how some teams try to perform. They relentlessly push to the objective and give and give. Until they can't anymore. Then they bite their nails wondering if they can get to the finish line before it is too late.

Teams that regularly elevate their High Performance Ceiling don't have DNA that predisposes them to having more energy than poor-performing teams. Instead, they have sustained strength, conviction, and enthusiasm because they focus differently.

Consequently, their focus generates a priceless resource: momentum.

If we're not careful, as a year progresses, jammed with endless meetings, conflicting priorities, and seemingly unrealistic demands to do more with fewer resources, something begins to happen: our focus changes. Once, we had the energy we needed to achieve big things. Then fatigue subtly shifts our focus to the widening chasm between where we stand and our target.

Because achievers get energy from *achieving*, confidence begins to break. Until the unthinkable happens: We begin to care less about achieving.

We must not relent in strengthening *how* and *where* we put our focus.

Staring endlessly at the chasm is career (and life) threatening. Momentum occurs when we lean forward. Teams experience this when they regularly place their focus on and celebrate the progress they're making. With the sense of achievement we become fascinated by the mystery in front of us, and we are driven by an energy that is seemingly not our own.

The next time the chasm of despair appears in front of you, ask these two questions to build momentum: 1) What is already working? and 2) How did we do that?

Strengthen this focus, and the momentum you'll experience is like getting free fuel for life.

Long Lever Questions:

1. How consistently and effectively do we create a sense of forward momentum by identifying what we're achieving?

2. Rather than assessing only that which we haven't done, how do we get better as a team at measuring that which we're achieving?

3. What's our plan to build greater momentum across our business with other teams with whom we partner?

What Are You Waiting For?

The fear of making a mistake is a greater motivator of inaction than the pain of living with others' errors. Some organizations are filled with people who will complain about the behaviors of others long before they ever act differently themselves.

What has to happen before people will collaborate more? When will a team function with increased trust? How do conditions have to change before people will be more transparent?

These are not rhetorical questions.

"I'm going to stay angry at you until you change" is not a strategy for improving team dynamics. (I've tried this approach and found the only change it creates is in my blood pressure.) If we wait for conditions to change before we change our behaviors, failure is certain.

Our responsibility to the team is to generate the conditions of excellence.

It's that simple: From our role we must be the initiator of productive outcomes.

The greater the number of people on a team who say, "I'll go first," the more likely the team will finish first. Our observations lead us to believe that the people who have the strength to initiate actions are motivated not by a desire to be seen as a leader. They are, rather, driven by a deep and burning conviction to always function with integrity to self, to the values they hold dear.

To not step up, speak out, and take action is to submit to a pain much greater than living with the pain caused by others' mistakes. As well, the achiever avoids the trap caused by criticizing others. This person's only measure, only judgment, comes from answering this question: Can I do more? And if so, what?

Others will judge you if you don't act. And they will judge you if you do. But only you answer to you.

What are you waiting for?

Long Lever Questions:

1. Where might we be rationalizing potential-stifling behaviors and poor performance – where we could be taking greater initiative?

2. When it comes to "generating the conditions of excellence," what are the expectations we have for ourselves? And are we meeting those expectations?

3. What sort of culture do we need to develop that further enables people to "go first"? And what's our plan to build such a culture?

What Will You Do When You're A Target?

Are you ready?

If you take action, if you step up and speak out, others will first interpret and then judge you. Biases and personal agendas mean they may even criticize you – with venom. "You're wrong!" they'll shout. "You're making a mistake and you'll pay!"

But they don't know what you know, do they?

In the moment after they're done pointing at you, and it's your turn to respond to their attacks, a tremendous opportunity for greater teamwork presents itself. Your ability to influence future cooperation will all depend on this:

Do you still respect those who appear to be your foe?

Those destined to be on mediocre teams, when judged by others, return the volley of judgment – and often with increasing intensity. They think they have to win and prove their attackers are villainous or less than they are. This "if-you're-not-with-me-you're-against-me" approach means they'll eventually run out of people who are willing to be with them. Consequently, they operate in increasingly smaller circles.

It's the other sort of response that builds a stronger team even in moments of conflict: We acknowledge the difference of opinion, forgive the attacker of his or her judgments, and focus on a virtuous outcome

Respecting others doesn't mean we agree with or even like them. It's simply an acknowledgment that we hear them and honor their right to have opinions. Doing so has a tremendous power and unifying effect.

The act of staying true to a vision will require us to step up, speak out, and lead.

And this will cause us to be targets of judgment and criticism. It's helpful, though, to remember that in the end there are few villains. Mostly, there are passionate people with diverse ways of living and leading. That, we can all respect.

1. What are the forms or acts of respect that we most value and feel are essential to our effectiveness as a team?

2. Where and in what situations can we do a better job of respecting those who have criticized our work?

3. What people, teams, or functions do we interact with that, should they experience greater respect from us, would likely mean we could expand our one-team approach with?

Big Ideas That Provide The Fulcrum Of Wisdom For Your Long Lever Questions

Activation Point: Perseverance

Top performers are no luckier than the average achiever. They don't have different circumstances – they have different behaviors. High-performing teams galvanize themselves with a mindset that filters circumstances, spending less time in frustration and more in inspiration.

Activation Point: Innovation

Loudly reject the claims of the cynics. They speak a language based in fear. Ask Long Lever Questions. Excellence isn't found in generating the perfect idea or solution, but in using your wisdom to deliver. When your instincts give you courage and inspiration, trust them.

Activation Point: Courage

Some cultures don't support team members who choose to be courageous by stepping up and speaking their mind. Breakthroughs in performance occur when we have the courage to develop an environment that rewards diversity of thought, when we are invested in the success of teammates, because relationships grow stronger in every interaction.

Activation Point: Leadership

Fixing problems isn't leadership, and it often creates problem people. Emotions rule over logic and reason. Leadership creates an improved future. It occurs when we address issues in ways that build and develop people and partnerships, thereby creating capacity and increasing potential.

Activation Point: Empowerment

There's a certain and undeniable link between the level of individual contributions on a team and the team's ability to succeed. Empowered team members realize a potential that is not confined to the limits of others' thinking. Developing capacity in others is rewarding and fulfilling for all.

Activation Point: Risk Taking

"Playing it safe" by not saying what needs to be said or doing what needs to be done lowers the High Performance Ceiling. Praise truth-telling, reward transparency, express enthusiasm for conflict in perspectives, and reward those whose failure prepares your team for success tomorrow.

Activation Point: Vision

We speak from pictures we see clearly in our head, and often assume others see the same image. This assumption causes confusion and poor performance. Discussions rich with questions create a language of excellence, because the team can then see the same thing – that which is necessary for success.

Activation Point: Momentum

A consistent focus on the chasm between where we are in our work and the distance to our targets creates despair and breaks confidence. How and where we place our focus is key. Celebration of what we are achieving ignites inspiration and provides priceless energy and momentum.

Activation Point: Initiative

Fear of making mistakes is a greater motivator of inaction than the pain of living with others' errors. If we wait for conditions to change before we change, failure is certain.

Our responsibility to the team is to generate the conditions of excellence. It's that simple: From our role we must be the initiator of things.

Activation Point: Respect

Taking action means you will be judged and sometimes criticized. Respecting others doesn't mean you agree with or even like them. It's simply an acknowledgment that you hear people and honor their right to have opinions. Doing so has a tremendous power and unifying effect.

Download a quick reference of all chapter summaries at
http://oneteambook.com/chaptersummaries

Where are we in our development of activating an inspired, one-team approach?

The following questions provide an opportunity to ensure your team is accountable to leveraging the wisdom and experience gained through Activation Points 12 through 21. As you record and reflect on your answers, compare your insights to those you recorded at the conclusion of Chapter Three. Consider the importance of the consistencies and contrasts in where your team was – and is now.

A. The strength of your team can and should be a model to other teams in the organization. Furthermore, if your team is truly committed to of leadership development, it's important to strategically identify how and where you can use your strengths to serve others. *In what ways are we taking what we're learning and applying it beyond our interactions with this team?*

B. Your team should be stronger than it was when you started reading this book, and therefore capable of working more effectively in overcoming obstacles. *What specific challenge is our team facing right now, and what have we learned through Part 1 of this book that we can immediately apply to create improved results?*

C. *What One Team behavioral competencies are we observing in ourselves on an increasing basis?*

D. *For these behavioral competencies to become "habit," what more can we do?*

Developing The Skill Of Using Long Lever Questions

Changing Your "Default" Questions

"I think of asking Long Lever Questions all the time," the senior manager, Sandra, said. Then with a smile she added, "Usually it's when the meeting's over and I wish I'd asked one."

Activating inspired teamwork requires developing new skills. Just as you didn't learn to ride a bike the first time you sat on one, so will asking Long Lever Questions require a new discipline.

At the end of Chapters Six, Seven, and Eight we'll provide you with three simple and proven techniques you can use to advance your capability in asking Long Lever Questions. For now, consider the following method that supported Sandra in creating a new "default" behavior while she was in meetings, one that enabled her to become more practiced in leading more effectively.

As we explored the process of her thinking, Sandra realized that her focus in most meetings was on the short term. Not surprisingly, when we interviewed her team, statements such as, "I always feel like it's a five-alarm fire with her – everything has to be done yesterday" were common. Inspired by Charles Duhigg's[3] superb book, *The Power of Habit*, we helped the senior manager identify her "cue," the moment she became aware that she was about to default to old patterns of behavior.Her cue was the feeling of stress (which she experienced more often than she cared to admit). Overwhelmingly, in these situations, she used short-lever questions with an interrogating tone:

1. Why did you do it that way?

2. When will it be done?

3. What will management think?

4. Why haven't you acted yet?

5. Any questions?

Next, upon realizing the cue, we encouraged her to focus on the "reward." Why was it important to her in these situations to shift to asking Long Lever Questions? For this manager, her motivation provided ample inspiration: She wanted to be the leader her team deserved. Additionally, more than just delivering improved results to shareholders, she wanted to realize a longtime vision: become super effective at developing future leaders around her.

With the cue and reward in place, the manager then needed replacement or "go-to" questions she could insert into the spaces where she was defaulting to short-lever questions. Here are three Long Lever Questions she memorized:

1. What is the most important thing we should discuss right now to more effectively move forward?

2. How do we leverage what we're discovering so that we're wiser for it in the future?

3. What is the value of our discussion, particularly as it relates to what we need to achieve?

"It was certainly awkward at first," she reported. Like anyone learning a new skill, she took uncomfortable

PREPARED LONG
LEVER QUESTIONS

pauses during meetings and periodically interrupted herself with statements like, "Wait, let me rephrase that" and "I'd like to ask a different question at this time."

Create Your "Starter Kit" of Questions

To advance her development, we established a process for vital feedback so the manager could quickly understand the impact of her efforts. Select team members were coached to strategically provide data to the manager after they observed her asking "new" questions: What resonated? What difference did the question make for the team? What could she have done even better? Why was it valuable to you that she was actively developing the new skill?

No surprise, like any achiever, this manager's persistence paid off. Six months later we had the opportunity to shadow Sandra again. Remarkably, upon investigating, we discovered that in just a matter of weeks she had moved past the Long Lever Questions she had memorized, and had begun to experiment by applying new inquiries.

The three questions she memorized might be considered a "starter kit." The Long Lever Questions you memorize can be entirely different than those outlined above. Also, consider:

1. What will be your "cue" that you've reached the moment when it's time to use your new go-to questions?
2. What's your "reward," the reason why you're willing to invest the effort to change your approach?
3. Who will you ask to provide sincere, specific, and selective feedback?

In short order, you will be on your way to developing a new habit, one that will differentiate you as a professional. In the end, however, perhaps that's not your biggest reason for asking Long Lever Questions.

CHAPTER SIX:

Driving
One-Team
Actions

The Discipline Of Teaming Forward

Energy isn't static. The power your team has, and direction you go, is determined by your collective focus. The essential skill for moving forward lies in the discipline of sustaining a forward focus. Does your team have it?

The mind can only focus on one thought at a time – and we go in the direction of that focus. Yet, while some teams say they want to move forward and deliver improved performance, their words and actions contradict their desires. Find any team that is consistently delivering mediocre results, and chances are you'll observe a group of people:

1. Endlessly analyzing problems.

2. Relentlessly exploring why ideas won't work.

3. Identifying who or what is to blame.

4. Consistently discussing what's not working.

The behaviors of your team are predictable, as they're determined by focus. Those teams with a discipline of success have a discipline of a forward focus. They seek facts, data, and information – and then deliberately choose a direction in their thinking that can only improve performance. In contrast to the list above, they proportionately spend more time:

1. Seeking solutions.

2. Determining how to make ideas work.

3. Identifying what can be learned from the past.

4. Leveraging what is already working

It is literally impossible to move forward if you're focused backward. This is not an encouragement to ignore problems. Quite the contrary. This is about how best to resolve problems.

Additional note: Having a forward focus is different from "thinking positively." For example, if my house is on fire, you'll not find me urging people to "be positive" and attempting to enjoy the experience. Rather, I'll have a forward-focused intensity for getting results: putting the flames out fast.

Long Lever Questions:

1. What's our philosophy concerning the type of focus and discussions necessary for sustained excellence?

2. How are we equipping ourselves to strengthen the discipline of functioning with this focus?

3. Where in the business can we become more disciplined in the forward-focused approach?

The High-Performance Discussion

Talking may be an aspect of communicating, but it alone doesn't qualify for having a productive discussion. Telling someone what to do over and over again is not effective dialogue. This prompts the question:

When we're having conversations . . . are we accomplishing anything important?

James Burns presented the idea of "transformational leadership" in 1978.[1] The idea (and we're respectfully taking the liberty of adding to his thoughts) is this: Individuals who use interactions with others to build and develop not just performance, but people and partnerships as well, consistently outperform employees whose days are filled with transactional, low-value exchanges.

The team that uses interactions to consistently shape and articulate a vision, and then executes toward that objective, is going to experience increased excellence. Here's how these High-Performance Discussions happen:

1. Team members go far beyond merely modeling behaviors of excellence; their thoughts are also consistent with their words and actions.

2. In their own language, they consistently message what's important and why. This ensures clarity of the path forward.

3. They develop ownership in others by <u>co-discovering</u> the most productive actions of excellence. Together, through questions, both the supervisor and employee learn.

4. Participants in the dialogue truly <u>listen</u> to one another (rather than trying to win an argument).

5. In the course of the discussion, as well as after, they stay true to the vision. This is done with a <u>focus</u> on what's working and what's next, rather than a derailing sustained focus on failures.

High-performing teams don't have time to waste in transactional interactions between one another. They use their moments of connection to build, to develop. Your authentic inspiration, blended with the elements of the High-Performance Discussion above, enables every interaction with others to be transformative.

Long Lever Questions:

1. To what extent are we seizing and leveraging daily interactions to get stronger as individuals and as a team? (Rather than just "going through the motions?")

2. Which elements of a High-Performance Discussion are we doing well? And where can we strengthen our interactions?

3. Why is it important to us as team members to maximize our interactions with one another?

Pathways to Leadership® Process Graduates:
Check out *ONE Team* resources exclusively for you in the
Graduate section of our website at: **http://verusglobal.com**

Is Your Approach What's Best For Results?

Many teams achieve – they just achieve something different than they wanted to. Clarity of intention and purpose are essential.

A primary example: *Collaboration is not consensus.* While these two words have entirely different definitions, we observe teams speak of the virtues of the former, and work tirelessly for the latter. They think they're collaborating . . . while they doggedly pursue consensus.

For many, collaboration means the ideas of multiple team members are solicited, yet a decision is subsequently made that some disagree with. Such a scenario can be risky for some teams, because one dissenter whose idea wasn't chosen can disrupt and derail the ability to execute the moment the team steps out of the meeting room. Yet, consensus takes time, and in some cases (particularly in those environments with high levels of politics) it's nearly impossible to accomplish.

The "we-can't-effectively-collaborate-but-can't-wait-for-consensus" scenario creates a conundrum. The market isn't patient.

This Activation Point is not an appeal to either method. It's simply meant to align on an understanding: To operate under the pretense we're being collaborative, when in fact consensus is what we're trying to achieve, disengages those who want to move faster. High-performing teams have a collective wisdom, and they give it voice: Are we looking for the best solution? Are we considering all ideas? Are we collaborating on this – or working toward total agreement?

Knowing which you're working to accomplish increases the likelihood you'll achieve what you want.

1. Which of the two methods – collaboration or consensus – have we generally worked toward in the past?

2. Under what circumstances do we favor collaboration? And consensus? And why?

3. What skills do we want to continue to develop in ourselves so that we can disagree with each other and still move forward "all in" and faster?

What If "What If" Happens?

Brilliant strategists didn't start out being that way. The leaders and teams that seem to have the right strategy at the right time often get their start by considering "what could go wrong?"

According to research by Collins and Hansen, found in their book, *Great by Choice*, companies that outperform others, especially in chaotic times, have "productive paranoia."[2] Strategic leaders and teams are disciplined in creating contingency plans to counter "what if?" scenarios. For example, what if we don't sell as many products as we anticipate? What if we sell more?

What needs to be emphasized in Collins and Hansen's argument is successful teams don't *sustain* a focus on exploring what could go wrong. Teammates who repeatedly utter, "Yes, but what if this bad thing happens?" can drive mad those who want to move forward faster. Without an important shift, "what if?" people are at risk of being branded as backward focused (and uninvited to future meetings).

The greater skill of strategic thinking doesn't lie in knowing what can go wrong; it's found in developing and delivering on a contingency plan. To accomplish this, our 180° Shift[3] technique has equipped leaders around the world to develop strategic thinking and actions within their teams:

180° SHIFT

Risks
Threats
Concerns
What I'm Worried About

Event

A. What's Important
B. Why
C. Forward Focus
Co-Discover Questions

Step 1: Identify the risk, threat, fear, worry, or what you don't want to have happen.

Step 2: State what's important to do or have happen and why it's important.

Step 3: Create greater ownership for the contingency plans by asking co-discover questions.

No one can predict the future, but you can influence it – and must, if you're to thrive.

1. What part of "productive paranoia" do we need to improve: considering "what could go wrong?" or crafting a contingency plan by messaging what's important to have happen and why?

2. How do we make sure our focus doesn't linger too long on what could go wrong – and we more effectively shift to what we can and should do about it?

3. What are some strategies we're currently benefitting from that began as contingency plans?

Take a deeper dive into the 180° Shift at
http://oneteambook.com/180shift
and experience videos and other resources.

What's In Your Future: A Collision or "One Team"?

Redesigning an organizational chart doesn't mean new teams are created, nor that increased productivity will be achieved. It simply means people have new positions and assignments.

Train wrecks happen everywhere: Like two locomotives racing toward one another, organizations acquire, merge, or create new "teams" – and then make little or ineffective investments for accelerating the conditions necessary for high performing teams. These forced collisions either deliver catastrophic results or require years before benefits are realized.

Predictably, when forced to work with others whom people have little or no relationship with, many individuals enter into a wicked, time-consuming "natural selection" process. Here's what it looks like:

1. Employees politic and position for prominence in the new pecking order.

2. Mistakes increase because "we-they" language is spoken, often years into the future.

3. Progress slows as personal and career safety requires people to "play it safe."

Without the tools to productively affect daily interactions early and consistently in the lifespan of a team, organizations strategically plan to fail. If you could build the alignment, communication, and trust in just a few days that typically requires years to "naturally" achieve, would you?

These are the successful actions we've supported teams in taking that ensure one-team performance is activated quickly after a redesigned organizational chart:

1. Rather than seeing which culture will "win," seize the rare opportunity to make two good cultures a great one by blending the best of both.

2. The extent to which people will work effectively together is determined by how well they know each other. Go beyond meet-and-greet parties and rope-climbing activities by equipping team members with relationship-building tools to inject into daily operations.

3. The company's motivation is clear: increase shareholder value. What is the motivation of each person in this grand play? Inspiration cannot be mandated; it's activated.

Bigger or different teams are only better when the ability to deliver value to the customer is improved. Be one team early and always.

1. What indicators appear when we are getting out of alignment? And what's our best response?

2. Historically, how has our culture been shaped? And how do we better influence it in the future?

3. When we add new team members, what's our plan to accelerate and *sustain* the alignment, communication, and trust necessary for success?

What It Takes To Be An Agility-Ready Team

Watch a competitive yacht team and you'll see excellence in agility. Despite a storm of rapidly changing currents or temperatures, or the team's deteriorating physical strength, they all fulfill their role in harmony.

Imagine if each time the wind, current, or another factor changed, the yacht team had to stop what they were doing, gather for a meeting, and make a plan for their response. Not only would they lose the race, the boat would likely capsize.

Business is done in a similarly stormy sea. The agility-readiness of a team, its ability to adapt to changing conditions with efficiencies and high-quality actions, is now a hallmark of highly productive teams.

It's painful to listen to management implore, "We must become more agile!" as if being so is merely an act of will. Agility is a skill that must be intentionally strengthened. Here's what it takes to be an agility-ready team:

1. Confidence and initiative: Team members who model courage take action not only in response to changes, but in anticipation of them. They see themselves as among peers – and are willing to go first.

2. Healthy culture: Put confident team members into strong partnerships with each other, where mindsets and behaviors are aligned with the team values, and you become greater than the sum of employees.

3. Full, free, two-way information flow: This element goes beyond simply "communicating" with one another. Because the team

members function as one, they receive and process data much like the five senses of the human body: in unison. Speed and efficiency is the result.

4. <u>Clear, achievable, stretch objectives and execution plan:</u> When we are aligned on what constitutes winning, where boundaries exist, and how we'll deliver with excellence, the conditions may change but we are unwavering in what and how we must achieve.

5. <u>A healthy team identity:</u> How we see ourselves, who we believe we are, is a powerful lens used to observe the world around us – and therefore respond to it. The paradigm of *"together we can"* is essential.

A world-class yacht team works to develop and ensure these five elements. The race is on. The choice is yours: Develop these essentials in every interaction of every day – or you can call another meeting.

Long Lever Questions:

1. In what important ways are we "agility ready"? And how is that driving high performance?

2. With what customer or project must we become more "agility ready"?

3. Which element from the list above will we focus on developing first – and why?

Data Rich, Knowledge Poor

The team can always make the case that we need more data. One more statistic, an additional assessment, get the facts – there's always more out there.

But does having more data mean we'll make a better decision? "We throw piles of data at people," a leader shared. "What we lack is knowledge." And knowledge is necessary for making good decisions.

Being data rich and knowledge poor is not a pathway to improved performance. It's akin to a kitchen filled with recipe books, but nary a dirty dish in the sink.

The temptation is to call meetings, discuss the numbers, and see where people want to go. "And when we do that," the same leader added, "we get exponentially more ideas and proposals. This results in the need for more meetings."

The question isn't whether or not to include people in the decision making. It's how to include and leverage people as you assess and disseminate data. It's worth discussing with your team:

1. What type of data would drive better and quicker decisions?

2. How much data do we need before we act?

3. As we assess the numbers, what organizational knowledge must we develop?

4. What knowledge do we need to develop so we can be more agile in decision making?

The exercise of collecting, possessing, and assessing data creates the illusion of knowledge. But success doesn't come to those who only know where they've been or what they need to do. Those who win model the courage to act and make new data points.

You are either reading data or creating it.

Long Lever Questions:

1. Of the discussion questions listed above, which should we explore and why?

2. Where might we be data rich and knowledge poor? And what would it look like to model being knowledge rich in those situations?

3. How can we improve sharing data more efficiently so that we can make faster and better decisions?

Beware The Team Hijacker

(Note: Hijacker is a loaded term, especially in this age of terrorism. Upon searching for a replacement word, however, we couldn't find one suitable for describing the effect on team performance when the progress of all is stymied by one person's refusal to change. Please accept our apologies for any unintended social-political faux pas.)

The individual who is richly talented, holds vaults of institutional knowledge, or has five-star relationships with key customers is only as valuable as his or her ability to align, communicate, and be trusted by peers. For a team to allow one of its members to function outside determined values, for the sake of retaining that person's technical skill, is a fatal error: The potential as a team is hijacked.

Choosing to believe we can't survive without a team hijacker is choosing to impose a low-hanging High Performance Ceiling.

The answers to these two questions create futures that are vastly different. "Can we survive without this person?" stands in significant contrast to this question: "What decisions must we make regarding this teammate to ensure we *thrive* as a team moving forward?"

A hijacker is only effective when we submit ourselves to a singular, limiting vision that there is only one way we can succeed. The team that searches for and executes solutions to the second question lifts their ceiling of potential much higher than those who only ask the first.

It's worth emphasizing that the hijacker is often not malicious or a bad person. In fact, the hijacker is often equally passionate about team success, if not more so. To blame someone else for slowing us down is to contribute to the dysfunction. There's a better approach.

Setting a new course forward that requires any sort of personnel change can be painful. It stretches most of us because we care about people. Yet, when we move beyond a dynamic that has restricted us, we discover a greater success *together*.

No one is bigger than all of us.

The reward for acting with this wisdom, from this value, is the fulfilling experience of being able to say: Together, we thrived.

Long Lever Questions:

1. Are we "walking the talk" and ensuring everyone is functioning at expected cultural standards?

2. How do we address hijacking situations in a manner that reflects our values?

3. In the future, rather than a focus of "fixing" a hijacker, what are the mindsets and behaviors we want to develop in daily interactions . . . so we increase our immunity to such dysfunctional dynamics?

A Call For A Certain Courage

"I used to see you walk around here on fire," a colleague tells another. "Now, you're as small as a pilot light."

Are you as inspired (as alive!) by your career and work as you once were? Integrity, the adherence to principles, is a supreme value in most corporations. Yet, our observations lead us to believe that the greatest violation of integrity in organizations goes unaddressed: the employee's integrity to self.

The system, and certain styles of leadership by those we are forced to follow, will harden us if we allow it to. Some around us in the organization succumb to behaviors we wouldn't tolerate in our children. They manipulate, they play king, they lie, they brag, they deceive, they blame, they hide.

When such actions are displayed by the few we may begin to suspect the whole. We will be tempted to quit believing that the majority is virtuous. When we refuse to cave to such small thinking, we realize a greater potential within ourselves for leading productive change – and become a model for those who wish to do the same. Most importantly, we remain in our own integrity.

This is not an appeal for a blind idealism. It's a call for courage over timidity.[4] Take decided action with the few who choose not to participate with integrity, while retaining enthusiasm for the whole. Doing so means we are true to who we are.

If you walk around as if you're on fire, if you're alive with the idea that most people want to do well for others, then we are with you. Your team will be with you.

Stay your course. Inspire those who are most certainly watching.

Long Lever Questions:

1. To what extent would you say others point at our team and say we "walk around on fire," inspired and acting with integrity?

2. How do we improve in our ability to take "decided action" with those not functioning with integrity, while remaining in our own integrity?

3. What shifts in our thinking and actions can we make so we can function on a daily basis with even greater integrity?

It Happens When You Elevate The Reason

He was shaking his head as he told us, "They can preach quality all they want. They can put checks and measurements in place every step of the way, but nothing big will change until people care."

"What would make people care more?" we asked.

"When they elevate our reason for doing the work well, beyond job security and delivering increased value to the shareholders," he answered.

People can't be forced to care, though they can be activated to do so.

The process of doing business, if not done thoughtfully, can squeeze caring from anyone. Consider this example: What does your team experience most as it innovates?

> **Step 1:** "Here's an IDEA . . ." moves to
>
> **Step 2:** "This is IMPORTANT . . ." becomes
>
> **Step 3:** "It's TIME SENSITIVE . . ." which slides to
>
> **Step 4:** "It's CRITICAL . . ." that now is
>
> **Step 5:** "URGENT" that can quickly collapse to
>
> **Step 6:** "FRANTIC," which is one step away from
>
> **Step 7:** "PANIC!"

Without focus and inspired leadership, new ideas signal another cycle of stress to those who have to deliver. (And we all have to deliver.) Slowly, "innovation" – an organization's lifeblood – becomes a dirty word. Talk of quality becomes synonymous with "keep your mouth shut," while more people slide further away from what they desperately want to do: care.

Quality work is an expression of self-worth. And that's something every team can build.

Long Lever Questions:

1. What do we believe people care most about in their work – and how is that related to our current levels of quality?

2. What type of culture has to exist for processes such as innovation to remain a productive, inspiring, and care-generating initiative?

3. To what extent do employees "own" our quality initiatives – and what can we do to further develop such a dynamic?

Big Ideas That Provide The Fulcrum Of Wisdom For Your Long Lever Questions

Activation Point: Focus
The behaviors of your team are predictable, as they're determined by focus. Those teams with a discipline of success have a discipline of a forward focus. They seek facts, data, and information – and then deliberately choose a direction in their thinking that can only improve performance.

Activation Point: Communication
Individuals who use interactions with others to build and develop not just performance, but people and partnerships as well, consistently outperform employees whose days are filled with transactional, low-value exchanges. High-Performance Discussions include modeling, messaging, co-discover questions, listening, and focus.

Activation Point: Collaboration
Collaboration and consensus are two different approaches to teamwork. Both are valuable; what's imperative is knowing which your team is attempting to use and achieve. Without clarity, frustration and failures mount; with understanding, efficiencies and effectiveness increase.

Activation Point: Strategic
Strategic leaders and teams are disciplined in creating contingency plans to counter "what if?" scenarios. Teammates who repeatedly utter, "Yes, but what if this bad thing happens?" can drive mad those who want to move forward

faster. Determine your "what if?" then make the 180° Shift by identifying what's important, why, and ask the co-discover questions.

Activation Point: Alignment
Bigger or different teams are only better when the ability to deliver value to the customer is improved. That is only achieved when the team is equipped to blend and strengthen cultures, build relationships with peers, and individual motivation and inspiration are activated.

Activation Point: Agility
Business is done in a stormy sea. The agility-readiness of a team, its ability to adapt to changing conditions, is now a hallmark of highly productive teams. Individual confidence, a healthy culture, information flow, achievable-stretch objectives, and an execution plan, along with a healthy team identity, are the essentials for developing an agile team.

Activation Point: Knowledge
Data-rich and knowledge-poor teams make slow or poor decisions. The question isn't whether or not to include people in the decision making. It's *how* to include and leverage people as you assess and disseminate data. You are either studying data or creating it.

Activation Point: Values
The individual who is richly talented, holds vaults of institutional knowledge, or five-star relationships with key customers is only as valuable as his or her ability to align, communicate, and be trusted by peers. No one is bigger than

all of us. Ask: "What decisions must we make regarding this teammate to ensure we *thrive* as a team moving forward?"

Activation Point: Integrity

The system, and certain styles of leadership by those we are forced to follow, will harden us if we allow it to. The actions of the few may cause us to suspect the whole. When we refuse to cave to small thinking, we realize a greater potential within ourselves for leading productive change. We remain in our integrity.

Activation Point: Quality

Quality work is an expression of self-worth. When we elevate our reason for doing the work well, beyond job security and delivering increased value to the shareholders – when we personally care – quality improves. People can't be forced to care, though they can be activated to do so.

Download a quick reference of all chapter summaries at
http://oneteambook.com/chaptersummaries

ONE TEAM PROGRESS ASSESSMENT

Where are we in our development of activating an inspired, one-team approach?

Inspect what you expect. Teams serious about continuing to improve their inspired teamwork can predict that they'll consistently elevate their High Performance Ceiling. The following strategic questions further enable your team to seize the potential they've developed, especially through the previous Activation Points.

1. What got your team here won't always get your team where it needs to go. It's wise to periodically revisit past decisions and, with new wisdom and perspectives, make necessary changes. *What team practice or decision have we made in the past as a team that we should now review or revise in a way that is more constructive?*

2. *As it relates to continuing to improve as a team, what public commitment can we each make?* Your challenge is to have each team member make a commitment that can be achieved soon, is measurable, and has an impact on results. These commitments should be documented, assessed, and moving forward, their achievement celebrated.

Successes from the Field

Would You Take This Job?

Adam wasn't sure he should take the job: Most think twice before accepting a role in an organization that has been failing miserably for years. Things weren't much better beyond the function, either. Overall, the company was on its heels, losing market share and receiving a steady stream of criticism from customers.

Adam, though, is not your average leader. He has a philosophy that gives him a unique confidence not typical at his level of leadership. "If it was just me that had to make this place great, we'd fail miserably. But it's not just me, it's the entire team. And I believe this team has tremendous, untapped potential."

Adam took the job. Because we're not writing a fairy tale, we can't say, "Adam never looked back. Never had any regrets." That wouldn't be true. The early days on the job were filled with misgivings and pangs of doubt that Adam had never experienced as a professional. It's moments like these that test one's values, character, and resolve.

The organization Adam is responsible for leading is supposed to develop innovative products for their company to take to market. We say "supposed to" because they weren't nearly as effective as they needed to be. Adam inherited a team that finished the year with a milestone success rate of 45 percent – a productivity score well below industry standards. To compound troubles, talented employees were fleeing the organization: Attrition stood at 12 percent.

"It was clear from the start that if we were to succeed in turning the ship around we had to unite the team – all 170 of them," Adam said. "We had to shift from a culture that was filled with ambivalence to one of ownership and confidence."

As we partnered with Adam, something important quickly became apparent:

Every person on the team, regardless of whether that person had direct reports, was a leader.

Adam made it clear that he expected team members to own their responsibilities, be leaders of self, contribute fully to the team, and drive organizational results.

How this was communicated to the team is worth highlighting. It's fair to say that most people in Adam's position would have spent a lot of time *telling* the team how they need to function. Adam's method for influencing the team, however, differentiates his leadership – and ultimately shaped the successes the team has delivered.

First, Adam made it clear what behaviors were important and why. Then, he asked Long Lever Questions.

Specifically, Adam discovered early that if team members were going to take greater ownership, one of the essential shifts to creating a breakthrough in performance centered on how information was shared among team members. Due to past experiences, people in the organization were conditioned to keep pertinent data to themselves, otherwise the material could be used against them. This is where Adam focused his attention.

Here's a sampling of the Long Lever Questions Adam asked. We're adding additional commentary in *italics* to emphasize strategic points:

A. "Trust is essential for any relationship to succeed. In the business environment it could be defined that both parties believe the other has their best interest at heart. What are some key behaviors that enable us to build relationships where we have trust at the center?"

Adam's use of strong platform or positioning statements prior to asking the Long Lever Question put the question into context. This enabled the team to be more specific in their answers.

B. "Transparent information is essential to our success as a team, because it provides us with the information we need to do our job. What are you discovering and learning that will better equip you to be more transparent when you're given the opportunity to do so?"

If you watch Adam in action, you'll observe these types of questions being asked not just in team meetings, but in one-on-one situations as well. These become prime and effective coaching sessions that occur in daily interactions.

C. "How can I better create a safe environment that enables you to be fully transparent?"

It's important to note that Adam didn't ask one of the most popular (and far weaker) leadership questions: How do I help you? Instead, he is very specific in what he is soliciting from the team.

D. "How does telling the truth quicker actually drive the performance we need to see?"

We're also excited about this question, and here's why: The answer may seem like common sense; however, it's repeatedly proven that by having people share their answers it increases the likelihood that common sense is put into common practice.

E. "What do you need from me and others on this team to have the confidence to step up and speak out when you have information we all need to succeed?"

Without context it would be difficult to comprehend the brilliance behind this Long Lever Question. Adam knew that in the past, people were punished for sharing bad news. Rather than asking a question that reminds people of pains and fears of the past, this forward-focused question better establishes a clearer path for future actions – and greater confidence.

F. "What is the culture you seek that will enable you to reach your true potential, and how can we facilitate creating that in this organization?"

Adam is walking the talk with this question. He knew he couldn't create the change by himself, so he's activating the vision and energy from the team. To do so, he's making it clear: We're co-creating something. My vision matters – and so does yours.

Perseverance pays. With each Long Lever Question Adam asked his influence reached deeper into the team. **He found what he suspected was there: brilliance.** Increasingly, the team began to take greater ownership. As they did, Adam gave them sincere, specific, and selective feedback that communicated his belief and gratitude for their efforts.

Adam now leads one unified and aligned organization where the individuals own and deliver on their responsibilities. As this book is going to press, Adam's team is at the halfway point of the year. Their milestone achievement rate is 100-plus percent. And employees are choosing to stay, as the attrition rate has plunged to 5 percent.

"You can move your score above 100 by delivering on your targets early," Adam shared with a smile. "And that's what the team has done. The momentum is noticeable to everyone in the organization."

Developing The Skill Of Using Long Lever Questions

3 Techniques For Developing The Skill

The business of improving a team's performance is the business of influencing others to take certain actions. Our research shows that overwhelmingly most people attempt to influence others by imposing information upon them: telling or commanding them to take certain actions, providing advice, and informing them of knowledge, among other techniques. However, these acts of putting content *into* another's brain are entirely different from the action necessary to extract or induce knowledge in the form of changed actions.

People demonstrate they've been influenced when they act upon the wisdom or new perspectives they have gained. Which begs the question: Are you busy making those around you smarter – or are you altering their actions that are necessary for success?

A growing number of leaders share our philosophy:

All team members are responsible for activating the potential around them.

People are responsible for influencing improved performance in those they interact with. A team that is equipped to "unpack" or activate the wisdom, experience, and knowledge in the people around them has an extreme advantage over teams composed of smart people who can't demonstrate their knowledge.

ONE Team has been designed with this thinking in mind. The book favors triggering or bringing forth changed actions in others. The Activation Points, and especially the Long Lever Questions, are tested and proven to put into action the intelligences and capabilities around you.

To supplement the actions your team is taking, we're going to complement the primary approach in this book. Now, and at the end of the following two chapters, we'll provide three proven techniques for constructing Long Lever Questions:

Technique #1: **Finish The Question**

Technique #2: **Focus On Values Over Tasks**

Technique #3: **Point At The Specific Issue**

There Is Short, Long, And Everything In Between

It's logical, and worth stating: There are varying degrees of Long Lever Questions. A question isn't short and then suddenly long with the change of a few words. Variations can be accomplished.

Here's an example of a short-lever question that gradually increases its leverage by continuing to build upon the original inquiry:

A. **What's next?**

B. **What's next** to improve this?

C. **What's next** to improve performance in a manner the customer wishes to see?

D. With the one-week window we have, **what's next** to improve performance in a manner the customer wishes to see?

E. With the one-week window we have, **what's next** to improve performance in a manner the customer wishes to see and that's done in a way that builds our brand image?

To reiterate, shorter-lever questions aren't bad. There are ample situations where it's appropriate to use questions in the form of A or B. The purpose behind learning and demonstrating the skill of asking Long Lever Questions is in response to the overwhelming evidence that:

1. At alarming levels teams are having discussions where there is little "turn-taking." This leads to de-activated employees.

2. High-performing teams require frequent patterns of communication, where team members step up, speak out, and lead.

3. Workplaces are often dominated by "power dynamics" that establish a low performance ceiling; this is characterized by a power that is used over people instead of for people.

4. In today's rapidly changing marketplace, teams are increasingly under pressure to perform, yet they are even more misaligned, functioning in silos or different geographical locations, and lack a common or shared objective.

With this wisdom in mind, let's explore how to construct a Long Lever Question.

Technique #1: Finish The Question

The first technique for constructing a Long Lever Question is one you can use in your next meeting or conversation. Our experience informs us that oftentimes the easiest method for creating a question with more power is to *finish* the question. This means instead of stopping with the "default" or "question of habit" we've asked for years, we simply complete the smaller question with elements that bring clarity and focus.

Let's apply this method to the sample questions taken from above.

"**What's next?**" becomes "**What's next** to improve this?" when we add the specifics we're seeking. The more detailed the question, the more thorough the responses. For example, the answer to "What's next?" might be the general answer, "We need to improve the project." Alternatively, "What's next to improve this?" will solicit specific ideas intended to do just that: improve what's being worked on.

Oftentimes, the best method to finish the question is by using a conjunction or word that joins two ideas. Here's a short list of conjunctions well-suited for creating Long Lever Questions:

A. So

B. And

C. Or

D. Yet

E. For

Consider this question commonly asked to focus others on execution: **How do we work our plan?** Here's how it could become a longer-lever question through the use of the conjunctions listed above:

How do we work our plan ...

A. ... **so** that the customer has greater confidence in us?

B. ... **and** prove we are fiscally responsible at the same time?

C. ... **or** redesign the plan for greater success?

D. ... **yet** reduce costs while doing so?

E. ... **for** purposes beyond current business needs?

Here's a challenge: Page through several of the Activation Points and identify where conjunctions are used to finish the second half of the question. Then consider: In what ways did the conjunction enhance the question – and how did that influence a more robust and productive conversation with the team?

CHAPTER SEVEN:

Accomplishing One-Team Accountability

It's Not The Time, It's The Performance Paradigm

Success can be disguised as "getting it all done," instead of delighting the customer. While these can be two different accomplishments, they're easy for achievers to confuse. Those who are programmed to achieve can slip and push to "do it all." But that's impossible. We discover our limits in the story we tell about time – a story that reveals how capable we are of high performance in the future.

These common statements rationalize poor performance and are easy to decode:

1. "I couldn't complete the project because I ran out of time."

2. "When I get home I never have enough time to exercise."

3. "We didn't have enough time to communicate with the other project team."

These messages all shout "I'm a victim."

Potential is de-activated when a team functions from the performance paradigm that the lack of time is the reason for failure. It's a convenient lie riddled with holes, including this fact: The competitor has the same bank of hours as we have. No more, no less.

"Time is the great equalizer," author H.L. Mencken said. More than that, it is the grand revealer, lifting the curtain so we can see who has the skill to achieve with the equalized resource.

Some organizations insist on how money should be spent, yet allow the resource of time to be spent at the discretion of the user without equipping the individual with means to align and prioritize. The resulting self-inflicted blunders cost money . . . and create the need for more time. At stake is the immense loss of personal fulfillment.

Top performers own their destiny. They seize responsibility because they know that aligning and delivering on priorities, communicating effectively with others, ensuring their personal physical health, and engaging with their family has little to do with time – and everything to do with their choices.

High productivity is less about the amount of time you have than it is about the performance paradigm from which you function.

It's not time that determines what and how much your team achieves. It's you.

Long Lever Questions:

1. As it relates to how we spend our time, where do we need to be more aligned on our priorities?

2. What are our agreed-upon decision criteria for how we spend our time?

3. What are our expectations for how we take and communicate responsibility for our use of time?

Delivering Consequences To Learn Success

High-Performance Discussions aren't meant for the purpose of creating comfort. Instead, they exercise the wisdom that our security lies in stretching, even being *uncomfortable*. When used, this language of excellence brings an unrelenting determination to succeed and an intolerance for mediocrity.

Consequences are feedback that should build capability in the team. Failure to administer consequences for successes or poor performance communicates to others a leniency or certain patience for realizing potential.

Often, in cases of poor performance, precious time is spent considering whether a consequence should be delivered. This can be a low-value conversation. After all, the choice was already made by the person whose behaviors and actions did not deliver the agreed-upon objective.

The more important discussion in moments of poor performance is the consideration of what the consequence is and how it is delivered. Done well, it is a powerful lever for development and growth.

Also critical is the difference between a consequence and a punishment. Blur the definition of these two approaches and leaders with the best of intentions can sabotage their own best efforts. A consequence becomes a punishment when:

1. It's delivered with anger.

2. It damages a person's development.

3. There's a perception of one winning at the expense of another losing.

4. We think we're using our power, but we're abusing it.

Consequences build capability when we:

1. Align on expectations. All parties share a vivid picture of what success looks like.

2. Respond to breakdowns in performance quickly.

3. Ensure consequences are a method for continuous improvement.

4. Administer consequences in ways that develop respect for all parties.

5. See excellence as the norm.

Fear, rigid policies, and punitive environments are the bane of high-performing teams. You welcome consequences that empower you and build your capabilities. This is another way excellence is learned.

Long Lever Questions:

1. In what ways might we be tolerating mediocrity that must be addressed soon?

2. How effective are we at delivering consequences that make people – and our team – stronger?

3. How do we become more effective at developing capabilities, so we don't have to rely as much on increasing punishing consequences?

Cream or Crud: What's Elevated in Your Organization?

An organization experiences success in proportion to the volume and type of information that is elevated up through the ranks of the hierarchy.

He who complains about having to deal with a stream of problems that come knocking daily at his office door may well consider the conditions creating the dynamic. To blame others for the inability to resolve issues is to model irresponsibility.

Some organizations are experts at knowing why they are failures. They elevate problems, study them, spend hours (or days) discussing them, and then resolve them in a way that guarantees more of the same tomorrow.

Teams that study successes, who understand why excellence happens, elevate and communicate solutions. This reduces destructive conflict. Importantly, the scope of possibilities and capacity widens for these organizations, which means they win more consistently.

To be empowered, and to empower others, is a skill. Rhetoric and pleas, two common approaches, won't develop this capability. High-performing teams address and take actions to resolve daily business issues – without burdening others. This is done by also aligning on the decision-making criteria for what issues do or don't get elevated. This infuses trust into other parts of the team or organization.

Our observations of effective leadership teams show clearly that those who find problems being elevated to them resist the temptation to play judge and weigh in with a verdict. Instead, they advocate for excellence by asking capability-building questions, including: "Based upon the data you have and your experience, what are your recommendations?"

The ability to respond and be accountable is a muscle. Today's problems are an exercise for tomorrow's excellence. Strength is essential to making sure cream, not something foul, rises to the top.

Long Lever Questions:

1. When you consider information we send up through the ranks, what's our current cream-to-crud ratio?

2. What capability do we need to develop so we can respond to our challenges with greater levels of responsibility?

3. What does it look like to trust each other as we model increased accountability to the areas of business for which we are responsible?

How To Support Peers through Change

It can cause premature aging: teammates facing organizational changes who won't budge or who even sabotage the efforts of others. We can stay younger by being aware of the focus others have, and consequently their energy and actions, as they move through a change initiative.

Author William Bridges expertly identifies three psychological phases everyone naturally goes through on an individual basis when experiencing change.[1] We're adapting his work and taking it a step further.

Phase 1: *Avoidance or Fear.* This commonly shows up as a backward focus characterized by defensiveness, procrastination, and reluctance meant to protect oneself. Expect to move slowly here.

Phase 2: *Indecisiveness.* This neutral mindset leaves one susceptible to ambivalence. One minute a person is enthusiastic about the change; the next moment he or she throws the project "under the bus." (And sometimes you with it.)

Phase 3: *"All in."* Now a person is almost entirely forward focused and is aligned with the new direction. People in this phase drive the change.

These phases are natural, and people move through them at their own pace. This is where some teams find themselves in unnecessary conflict: Some people expect others to be where they are in the phases of change. Criticism, demands, and persuasive lectures often follow, leaving the entire team focused on the disablers who are slowing the change effort.

Teammates who are serious about one-team high performance *serve* their peers by assisting them through any phase of change and the emotions inherent in the effort. It can look like this:

Step 1.　Show empathy for others' current state.

Step 2.　Articulate the vision (co-create it when possible).

Step 3.　Tap into the motivations of each individual.

Step 4.　Identify each person's role.

Step 5.　Ask questions for co-discovery and learning.

Step 6.　Provide feedback on progress.

Long Lever Questions:

1. Consider a current initiative. Where are we in the phases of change? What's our rationale?

2. What are some actions we take that possibly backfire and keep people stuck in phases 1 and 2?

3. Using steps 1 through 6 above, how will we better support others through the phases of change?

The Perfect Team To Succeed

It stinks. It's tough. We're doomed either way. (How do we get out of this?)

Wait.

What if . . . we're perfect for this situation? What happens if everything we've ever done and decided . . . has brought us to this moment – and we're the *perfect* team to move this woeful situation forward?

An executive team we work with had to change their organization's business model because the company wasn't making money. The new model meant fewer employees. (Still, it would result in more employees than if they went out of business.) Some people, whom they recruited and who uprooted their families to join them, would be let go. The pain was palpable.

You know people like those on this leadership team. They're your neighbors and friends – good to the core. They're exceptional human beings facing difficult and extreme circumstances.

Their choices? Be victims. Delay the inevitable. Crumble. Question their ability.

Or...be accountable.

Inspired teams don't see accountability as a choice.

It's an obligation. Modeling their values is

the only option. Therefore, they have the presence, humility, fortitude, focus, empathy, vision – the courage – to take responsibility. They may not want to do what has to be done, but they're the perfect team to do it *right*.

The team identified above delivered on their plan: They improved business performance in a manner that modeled empathy, fostered two-way information flow, and developed greater trust with each employee.

Your team possesses all the right people to fail. You also have all the right people to succeed.

The reason your team is in the position it's currently in is to prove you're the perfect team for the job. Be accountable to the greatness you possess.

Long Lever Questions:

1. What is it about our team that gives us the confidence to know we can persevere and succeed?

2. What does accountability look like when we are faced with choices where no options are desirable?

3. Where in the business, and in what ways, can we be more accountable individually and collectively?

Getting Friendships Right

Teams that have "aged" nicely (where the members have worked together for many years) can find themselves in a conundrum:

When a performance issue arises can the truth be told? And can the truth be *acted* upon?

For longtime friends the lines of loyalty can be blurred and challenging to navigate. What's more important: achieving the team objective – and in the process having a truth-filled conversation with a friend, or protecting ourselves or those we've been in the trenches with for years – by avoiding the reality of current business results and necessary action steps forward?

Friendships are a powerful mechanism for performance. Caring for others deeply means we're more likely to be accountable to one another. This bond and trust is essential for a team to accelerate through the darkest challenges.

The strongest friendships, though, create (often demand) a fierce loyalty. And that's where the rub is. When loyalty to a person takes priority over our loyalty to the mission of the team, trouble ensues: The truth isn't told. No team member, no isolated relationship, is bigger than the shared purpose of the team. Effective teammates know where this line is and won't cross it because the cost is potential lost.

Dishonor goes to those bosses who disregard the friendships that have been built by not searching for ways to honor and leverage the loyalties of friends for the greater cause. For it is on the backs and in the hands of those we've gone to battle with that we are indebted.

Honor is earned by those whose loyalty is revealed to friends by telling the truth *early* and clearly. "Our friendship and my loyalty to you is so strong, I *have* to share this information and perspective with you." Then, two teammates emerge aligned and better capable of delivering on their shared loyalty.

Long Lever Questions:

1. Where do our loyalties to friends and our mission converge and diverge? How can we better recognize such moments?

2. What does it look like for us to have a collective awareness of, and professionalism around, this issue?

3. What does it mean to be "all in" for each other in those moments when we're not delivering on our standard of excellence?

For more resources on supporting friends in the workplace, visit
http://oneteambook.com/loyalty

One Word To Achieve More: No

Achievers will go to extreme lengths to achieve success. Missing opportunities, angering a boss, or being perceived as inadequate are not options. So we say "yes." We say yes to more; yes to a wrong; yes to the impossible. And ironically, in saying yes when we shouldn't have, we experience consequences more significant than if we'd originally said "no."

No: It's the one word – when articulated effectively – that frees a team to achieve more.

"No" has earned a bad, and often unfitting, reputation. Too often it has stopped progress or limited opportunities. This angers those who want to see improved productivity. As well, saying no is perceived as a rejection of the person who brought forth the request or idea. Because most people are programmed to please others, the conundrum becomes clear.

A team's ability to achieve the new is in proportion to their ability to refuse the unnecessary.

A team's refusal rate, therefore, is one worth celebrating.

The solution lies in using "no" as a beginning, rather than an ending, then coupling it with forward-focused questions that launch new opportunities:

A. "No, given the current commitments we have, we won't take on that project. How do we better prioritize our current objectives so we can also meet expectations in other areas?"

B. "No, we won't partner with anyone who puts our brand at risk. How do we collaborate more effectively so we both win?"

C. "No, we can't stay quiet. How do we move forward with greater transparency?"

D. "No, I won't allow us to dwell on non-value-add discussions. What are the forward-focus questions we can use in this situation?"

E. "No, I won't attend that meeting. I trust the decisions the team makes, because . . ."

"No" is a powerful, forward-focused tool when it activates a more significant potential.

Long Lever Questions:

1. Why is it essential that we get better at incorporating no into our language of excellence?

2. What are some projects we can say no to now – and also add questions to launch improved solutions? (And what would those questions be?)

3. In the future, when a team member says no, what is going to be our healthy response?

Does The Competition Fear You?

Manuel's team was "committed," yet in the end they failed. In hindsight, Manuel told us, he realized why: The word had become an empty pledge. Team members acted like they were committed when there was a crisis. When there was no emergency, though, there was no urgency. Their level of commitment was a condition of circumstances in the business.

For those devoted to one-team excellence, commitment is unconditional.

These teammates function "all in" consistently and early. Like a card player who slides all his chips into the center of the table, they're not waiting to give their best efforts only when the cards are right. Nor do they hide chips under the table in reserve. Instead, they're 100 percent all in with their efforts 100 percent of the time.

Teams composed of people such as this cannot be beaten by competitors who merely have more talent. A force greater than the sum of the individuals is required to win this contest.

The Activation Points in *ONE Team* build the awareness and inspire the discussions that further enable each of us to be "all in *early.*" This means we don't wait for a teammate to be in need before we assist. We are all in *before* the requirement of extreme efforts arises. This is the only way to reduce the effect of crisis we will face in the future.

Each team should collectively define what it means to be "all in *early.*" Those who have gone before you found it useful to first align on what "all in *early*" is not:

1. It doesn't mean we always agree with one another.

2. It's not a method to protect people from honest and high-performance discussions.

3. It's not a signal that I'm on board with an initiative.

What does "all in *early*" mean to your team? As you answer, does your definition:

1. Make clear that every interaction among team members should be used to develop capabilities and strengthen partnerships?

2. Enable people to be fully transparent and open to feedback from others?

3. Drive the link between daily actions and corporate values, targeted leader competencies, and business objectives?

Being a contributing member of a high-performing team is a deeply personal choice. Identifying and leveraging *why* we want to be "all in *early*" changes our collective game in a sustainable way. Ultimately, the greatest reward is also personal: By realizing our own potential we activate the team's greatness.

Long Lever Questions:

1. What is our definition of what it means to be "all in *early*"?

2. How do we get better at demonstrating being "all in *early*"? (Rather than waiting for a crisis.)

3. What are our personal motivations for wanting to function, lead, and contribute this way?

What It Takes To Be A Legend

On a recent flight I sat next to a professional rodeo bronc rider. Imagine making a living sitting on a crazed horse that has one objective: kicking you to the stars.

I asked him: "Okay, if I ever find myself on a bronc, what are the three things to remember if I want to be legendary?" His answer transcends his sport and advises any team wanting to break their High Performance Ceiling:

1. "**Stay in front of the horse.**" You must be *more aggressive* than the crazed beast that's bucking, twirling, and fuming. When you get behind your horse, it's a rough ride. It's no fun. And you don't score points.

2. "**You score more points when the horse is strong.**" You want the horse to buck as violently as possible. (If the horse is weak and you look great on it you still won't win.) Then, remember point #1.

3. "**You're not competing against the horse. You're competing *with* it.**" The horse has no interest in working with you, but when you work with it, you can win.

Business is like a bronc. Every rider gets thrown from the horse from time to time. To win requires endurance and sustained effort. Of what courage are we built?

Hope for a strong ride so you can score points, be more aggressive, stay in front, and work with the force of the business. Go be a legend.

Long Lever Questions:

1. How have we proven that we have what it takes to endure, sustain our focus and effort, and persevere?

2. We're on a bucking bronc! How do we get better at framing that as a productive thing in our daily work? And why is doing so important?

3. How do we know if we're competing against the business – or with it? And what does it look like to make this shift successfully?

Don't Be The Reason Your Team Fails

(Not very inspiring, is it.)

Consistent fear leads to failure consistently.

"I came from a culture where there was a general mandate: Don't be the reason we don't succeed," a manager shared with his new team. "It didn't prove to be a model that motivated us to excellence."

Fear as a management technique motivates, but not for long. Used excessively, the erosion of quality, innovation, and everything else high-performing teams covet is severe. When is using fear as a leadership lever worth the payoff? The answer is worthy of careful analysis.

Additionally, leaders can unknowingly or inadvertently silently "scare" those they lead. Without knowing it, our words, decisions, and actions can induce trepidation, resulting in a team that moves like a car creeping into an intersection long after the light has turned green. Or the opposite occurs: Alarms are sounded and the team runs through stop signs.

It behooves us to periodically examine how our leadership may inadvertently de-motivate others. However, asking, "What are you afraid of?" is unlikely to inspire the masses to be intrepid. Instead, try Long Lever Questions such as these to address any "silent" fears and further motivate the team:

1. If we could shed any potential consequences for taking this action, what would those consequences be?

2. What are three shackles we'd have to remove for us to be fearless in this situation?

3. What tends to be the top risks we avoid that, if they were removed, would activate greater performance?

Cultures of fear, including those that point blame at others, fail. Cultures of responsibility, where people can step up and speak out – "I'm responsible for the failure" – win.

To fear is human. To overcome it is courageous. To replace it with inspiration is leadership.

Long Lever Questions:

1. What are some of the (un)spoken fears our team harbors that limit excellence?

2. Are we simply asking people to be courageous – or are we equipping and developing others to replace fear with virtues necessary for success?

3. What will it look like for us to more consistently function as an intrepid and inspired team?

Big Ideas That Provide The Fulcrum Of Wisdom For Your Long Lever Questions

Activation Point: Time Management

High productivity is less about the amount of time you have than it is about the performance paradigm from which you function. It's not time that determines what and how much your team achieves. It's you. Top performers own their destiny. They seize responsibility.

Activation Point: Discipline

Consequences are feedback that should build capability in the team. Failure to administer consequences for successful or poor performance informs others of lenience or certain patience for realizing potential. There is a critical difference between a consequence and a punishment.

Activation Point: Empowerment

An organization experiences success in proportion to the volume and type of information that is elevated up through the ranks of the hierarchy. To be empowered, and to empower others, is a skill. Today's problems are an exercise to develop the muscle for tomorrow's excellence.

Activation Point: Change

People move through the three psychological phases of change at their own pace: Avoidance or Fear, Indecisiveness, and "All In." Unnecessary conflict occurs when people expect others to be in the same phase as they are. Teammates on high-performing teams serve their peers by assisting them through the phases.

Activation Point: Accountability

Inspired teams see accountability as an obligation. Therefore, they have the presence, humility, fortitude, focus, empathy, vision – the courage – to take responsibility. They may not want to do what has to be done, but they're the perfect team to do it right.

Activation Point: Loyalty

Friendships are a powerful mechanism for performance. Strong friendships, though, often demand a fierce loyalty. When relationships take priority over the mission of the team, trouble ensues. Honor is earned by those whose loyalty is revealed to friends by telling the truth early and clearly.

Activation Point: Refusal

"No" has earned a bad, and often unfitting, reputation. It is a powerful, forward-focused tool when it activates a more significant potential. The solution lies in using "no" as a beginning, rather than an ending, then coupling it with forward-focused questions that launch new opportunities.

Activation Point: Commitment

Commitment is unconditional for those devoted to one-team excellence. These teams function "all in" consistently and early. Like a card player who slides all his chips into the center of the table, he's 100 percent committed all the time. He delivers best efforts *before* the requirement calls for extreme efforts.

Download a quick reference of all chapter summaries at
http://oneteambook.com/chaptersummaries

Activation Point: Endurance

Business is like a bronc. To win requires endurance and sustained effort. Be more aggressive than the forces in play, embrace the strength of your circumstances, and work *with* the force of the business – not against it.

Activation Point: Motivation

Cultures of fear, including those that point blame at others, fail. Cultures of responsibility, where people can step up and speak out – "I'm responsible for the failure" – win. To fear is human. To overcome it is courageous. To replace it with inspiration is leadership.

ONE TEAM PROGRESS ASSESSMENT

Where are we in our development of activating an inspired, one-team approach?

1. *On a scale of 1 to 5 (5=Strongest), to what extent are we delivering on our commitment of consistently developing one-team behavioral competencies? And what's the rationale for our score?*

2. *To ensure we remain grounded in our motivations, what were the reasons why further developing our one-team approach was important to each of us?*

3. *As we become stronger together, where are we seeing the effects outside our team? What are the implications of these outcomes?*

Developing The Skill Of Using Long Lever Questions

3 Techniques For Developing The Skill:
Technique #1: Finish The Question
Technique #2: Focus On Values Over Tasks
Technique #3: Point At The Specific Issue

Long Lever Questions present a tremendous opportunity to inspire people, including ourselves. This is accomplished because these types of questions elevate thinking and connect us with an even greater cause.

Take this Long Lever Question as an example: "How do we work our plan and prove we are fiscally responsible at the same time?" For the manager unpracticed at the skill of asking Long Lever Questions, it would have been easy to ask a question that focuses on the task: "How do we come in under budget?" This is a default question we often hear in the workplace.

Consider, though, that most professionals already know they have to come in under budget. Certainly those who have a record of achieving know this. Defaulting to and repeatedly asking such "task" questions invariably dampens enthusiasm for the job.

There's greater opportunity in this moment, and asking the better question seizes the potential that always exists. Standing for something important, modeling our character, demonstrating that we are worthy – these are all calls to inspiring action. Coming in under budget? That's what the average team does. Showing that we can be counted on to be fiscally responsible means we reveal a bit of who we are as a team. This earns greater trust moving forward.

One COO at a global company in the food and beverage industry put it this way: "Focusing on and incorporating values and leadership behaviors into our daily conversations means we don't have to manage every interaction people are having."

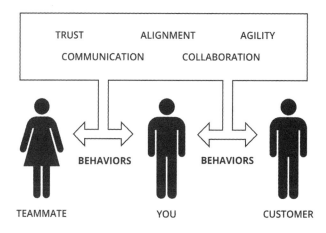

She's right. Behaviors are born from values. When a team is aligned on the values, the diversity of behaviors aligned with those values creates the differentiating strength a team needs to succeed.

For other examples of Long Lever Questions that focus on values over tasks, flip through any of the Activation Points listed in this book.

For instance, consider the Activation Point titled "Only For Teams With Guts," in the appendix. Here are the three Long Lever Questions that accompany this point:

1. To what extent is our level of effort contingent on the actions of others?

2. What motivates us to relentlessly give our best, regardless of the circumstances around us?

3. What does it look like to "have someone's back" even when we disagree with that person's approach?

Question 1 is an awareness-building question designed to align a team on current skill levels. The answers to this question alone have led to breakthrough thinking. Yet, we chose to take discovery further in questions 2 and 3 by tapping into certain values that are consistent with one-team performance.

In these questions we didn't specifically name the value, though. That's something you as an agile team member can do if you want to add even greater specificity. For example, imagine that "Effective Collaboration" is a value for your organization. This means that question 3 could be restated this way:

"What does it look like for us to effectively collaborate even when we disagree with each other?"

A focus on values elevates thinking as it connects closely with one's purpose.

This empowers people to be a greater expression of who they want to be. Long Lever Questions are a tool to accomplish this.

The Purpose Is To Activate

The best Long Lever Questions activate and convert potential into greater reality sooner. They move people, partnerships, and performance forward. This doesn't mean, however, that the Long Lever Question should have a word count that requires a coffee break half way through it. As well, Long Lever Questions are not an excuse to cram numerous short-lever questions into the same query.

Consider this Long Lever Question: "With the one-week window we have, **what's next** to improve performance in a manner the customer wishes to see and that's done in a way that builds our brand image?" If not asked and timed well, it could be considered a run-on sentence and confuse people.

There are, though, specific instances when this very question has proven to be exactly what's necessary to inspire tremendously effective teamwork. In these and similar cases, leaders have been encouraged to pause strategically throughout the question as they ask it. It might sound like this:

"With the one-week window we have, **what's next** to improve performance in a manner the customer wishes to see and that's done in a way that builds our brand image?

CHAPTER EIGHT:

Activating
One-Team
Inspiration

What Causes Us To Give More

When we belong to something bigger than ourselves we are, as individuals, called to do more. Pride – the sort that goes beyond self – is priceless. When this occurs the members of a collective endeavor get something back in return for their efforts that can't be purchased with money.

Is the reason your team exists worth the effort you're asking people to give?

Is the cause worth the discretionary effort?

Making more money for shareholders (many of whom most employees will never share a cup of coffee with) may be how we keep score. And earning an income is certainly worth hard work. But we fool ourselves thinking most people will sustain a level of motivation – of inspiration – and work harder just to make more money. Studies repeatedly show this approach is inadequate for getting the best from others.[1]

A team that bonds together and sees themselves as one of a kind will deliver one-of-a-kind results. But how do you develop that sort of pride in an era when who's on the team can change faster than a teenager updates her favorite social media page?

Stories build this type of pride. People listen and relish telling them. When a teammate recounts the best of the past, they share knowledge and transfer institutional wisdom in ways that corporate policy and manuals never can.

Tell me a story . . .

1. . . . of other periods in our team's history when change was managed well.

2. . . . of the people who best model our key values.

3. . . . of when you've seen this organization persevere through hardships – and how it was done.

High-performing teams believe excellence is what they *do*. This paradigm is reinforced when we tell stories that remind us we are better together than we would ever be apart.

Long Lever Questions:

1. What do we gain, beyond a paycheck, by being a part of this team?

2. What are some of the stories we want to reinforce in our culture – and for what purpose?

3. Given our current challenges, what sort of stories do we want to tell now and in the future?

What Are You In The Business Of Doing?

What are you providing that the market wants? Maybe you're in a different business than you originally thought you were.

"I'm clear with my team," a VP told us. "We are in the business of developing leaders – at all levels and in every role. That's our responsibility to the company. It's the quality of our leaders that determines the quality and volume of the product we ship. It's the strength of our leadership that will determine how fast we can grow."

This sort of thinking isn't common. Most organizations have a DNA formed from generations doing business where there was only one leader per team. The rest of us followed. Now, those days are gone. (If you don't think they are your job may well be gone soon.)

The emphasis on lean, the elimination of waste, and the squeezing expectations of shareholders mean that one person is now responsible for the job several did yesterday. Each employee is exposed to expectations and responsibilities never imagined years ago. To lament this is to waste time fighting a current that isn't changing direction.

High performers see an important reality: There have never been more opportunities to excel and differentiate oneself. The VP above is excited: Before, he was only concerned with continuously improving the product he shipped.

Now, developing leadership, talent, and team have an equal share of the spotlight; the growth in these areas drives the improvements in the product.

This profound change is calling all of us to become more effective at fulfilling our potential as people. We must further shed the conditioning of hundreds of years that says we are only meant to follow. We must trust our instincts and step forward. We all must activate potential from our respective roles. Shared leadership is no longer a destination, it's the path forward.

When you are in the business of developing leaders and building high-performing teams, the market wants more of what you offer.

Long Lever Questions:

1. What are we in the business of doing? And where does developing leaders and great teams fit in that answer?

2. What's our ratio of followers to leaders? And what's the relationship of that ratio to our current level of success?

3. How do we measure a team member's ability to activate high performance in those around her?

Where Are The Borders For Your Team?

Mastering the ability to activate one-team performance is an achievement worth celebrating. Still, a team that functions in isolation of, and out of sync with, other teams in the enterprise remains short of its true potential.

Additionally, in today's organizations, employees have multiple reporting channels, each of which are competing for the time and attention of the individual. Confusion is common and stress is particularly intense when, without care, false boundaries for teams are established. The limits imposed by these definitions establish the confines of organizational productivity.

Where does the border of your team lie? What's the extent to which you define your "team"?

It used to be enough to complete your task and then throw the widget over the wall for the next functional team to complete their chore. Now, in order for any organization to deliver successfully, you are required to work in parallel with people you may not know (and may never see).

Let's take it a step further: Today, employees are often required to team with people who don't get a paycheck from the same source. Under such circumstances teamwork isn't achieved through platitudes or slogans; such empty approaches are manipulative. One-team performance is only achieved when the accountability two parties have to a shared cause transforms into a responsibility to one another.

High-performing teams develop effective partnerships

beyond the traditional boundaries of their team, thereby expanding the border of their influence.

They seize seemingly mundane interactions to create the conditions that form and nurture strong *relationships*.

If you want to build accountability in others, build relationships with them. The strength of the connection between people predicts the level of accountability between people.

Today you are a part of a borderless team.

Long Lever Questions:

1. How effectively do we activate one-team performance as we partner with other teams and functions beyond our traditionally defined "team"?

2. What are the "conditions for strong relationships" we know we need to develop with others outside our immediate team?

3. Which behaviors found in the Activation Points in this book will we use to build high-performance partnerships with others?

The Michelangelo Approach To High Performance

People are looking for solutions to problems they've never seen before. (If you're seeing the same problems, you've got other issues.) Be careful where you look for answers.

Do you believe success lies outside your team – or within it? The artist Michelangelo once said, "Every block of stone has a statue inside it and it is the task of the sculptor to discover it."

There is genius within your team. The key question is: What are you doing in every team interaction to further activate the inherent genius?

Teams that experience a perpetual focus on their problems are prone to inaccurate beliefs: We are incomplete – or worse, broken. We lack greatness. To get "there" we must go out and purchase and acquire something to make ourselves better. This mindset is an invitation for exhaustion: You have to wait for tomorrow to be successful.

Don't buy the bull. Today is your team's moment of excellence.

The past has prepared you perfectly for what has to be accomplished now.

If you believe you don't have what's necessary to succeed you are choosing to fail. Excellence isn't an outcome, it's an action. The solutions to the problems we've never seen before begin to reveal themselves as we become better at being who we believe we can be.

Resist the temptation to criticize or lament your limited resources (the stone before you); instead, do what Michelangelo did:

1. Know your peers want to deliver excellence.

2. Be more forward focused than not.

3. Build accountability by developing partnerships.

4. Routinely solicit the ideas and honor the motivations of others.

Replace the doubt. The formula for success lies in relentlessly improving who you already are. You can do this.

Long Lever Questions:

1. What would it look like to consistently function knowing we can – or will – succeed?

2. What elements of a high-performance masterpiece can we get stronger at building?

3. What is the inherent genius within our team that we should further reveal?

Four Categories Of Questions That Facilitate Change

Kings and queens didn't want their subjects to think. Leadership beliefs of that bygone era still persist well beyond the industrial age: Society is still plagued by a belief that it is a select few who make the decisions, while the rest of us are meant to wait and do only as we are told.

Times are changing. The information age and "connection economy," as author Seth Godin calls it, are driving a new model of teamwork: The length of time a team waits to be told what to do is in direct proportion to an organization's profitability. The teams who are proactive deliver on their potential. They enable their organization to win more consistently.

How do you get people to take initiative, think, and act?

"People will do remarkable things when you ask them," said Jack Stack, author of the timeless book *The Great Game of Business.*

What sort of questions have the greatest influence on developing proactive behaviors?

Our research shows these four categories of questions are essential to improved performance:

1. *Alignment, Objectives or Vision questions,* such as: What does success look like? What is our shared objective?

2. *Execution questions,* such as: What needs to be done? How do we deliver on the objective?

3. *Motivation questions,* such as: Why is accomplishing this important as it relates to our objectives? What do we ultimately want to achieve?

4. *Accountability questions,* such as: How will we measure our progress? What milestones will ensure the delivery of your plan?

In combination with clear directions of what's important and why from those with the responsibility of giving direction, these questions ensure the conditions for accelerated change are met. The influential power of these inquiries lies in the fact that they are co-discover questions that result in people learning together. Now everyone is thinking. There's no manipulation of one person over another, only exploration of an improved path forward as both parties explore answers.

You can be the team that prevails over those ruled by kings and queens.

Long Lever Questions:

1. Of the categories of co-discover questions, which should we get better at asking – and why?

2. What outcomes will we see as evidence that we are asking ourselves and others more effective questions, such as those provided as examples?

3. Why is it important to us as a team that we improve our ability to ask better questions?

After We're Done Criticizing Each Other

You're too loud. He's too meek. She doesn't understand.

You don't have enough experience. She's too forceful. He's inauthentic.

You're too American. You're too European. (You're too . . . where are you from?)

He's too pragmatic. She's not a realist. They don't get it.

You're too enthusiastic. They're not responsive enough.

(And who hired you anyway?)

After we're done criticizing each other (telling ourselves why "we can't" achieve), we get to make a decision:

Are we going to win together or fool ourselves into thinking we can persevere separately?

Any study of great teams shows that the members of those teams spend little time minimizing teammates. (In fact, they won't tolerate it.) Together, they ask for – in fact, they insist on – people being the truest expression of who they are. They don't require people to be less; they ask for more in a way that delivers the mission of the team.

Collective potential is left un-activated when a team gets less than the best from any of its members. Who we really are when we're allowed to be ourselves is one of a kind. Accomplish this collectively as a team and we amplify a brilliance that differentiates us – which is ultimately what the market is demanding.

1. What does it look like for us to go beyond tolerating the differences in others, to actively cultivating those differences?
2. How and in what situations are we effectively honoring and leveraging our diversity?
3. Where and in what ways can we admire, respect, and "have each other's back" even more?

Bonus: Is honoring diversity *really* important to us? And if so, why?

The Human Spirit Was Not Meant To Conform

Most of us want to be a part of an inspired workforce, yet many participate in and develop a compliant one, which squelches the connection between person and purpose. People can hardly be blamed. As children, for example, the system pressed us to conform, so we played "follow the leader" and other games with our peers. Work systems everywhere continue the trend.

To be sure, compliance has its place: safety, quality, and regulations top the list. The preaching boss, however, who demands or uses manipulative tactics to gain the compliance of her subjects is in many respects weak. She falsely believes that leading a compliant team is easier than inspiring one. (*"Want to keep your job?"* Yeah, I thought so.) It is, however, much more difficult to force people to do a job than to guide those who are willingly stepping up, speaking out, and taking action.

The human spirit was not meant to conform. Inspired self-expression, both individually and as a team, brings with it a boldness that smashes through the productivity levels of the compliant workplace. This is the environment high performers are desperately seeking. This is the environment of which we want to be a part.

To succeed in this hyper-competitive and lean age of business, people have to matter. And why they matter is not just because of what they can do, but also because of who they can be. As more teams function in ways where team members activate greatness in each other, inspiration, and its cousin, commitment, become norms.

Yes, some of us work for managers who are loath to embrace inspiration as a means to achieve excellence. Meanwhile, to forfeit our inspiration –

our responsibility to ourselves and each other – won't do. We choose to wake up each morning and be committed to a cause greater than we are. We choose to express our values, including a work ethic that informs the world who we are: inspired.

A team achieves excellence when they're inspired by the notion of experiencing it.

Long Lever Questions:

1. In the work we do, what does it look like to function more consistently from an inspired state?

2. In our daily interactions, how do we want commitment to be demonstrated – and why?

3. Why do aspects of our work inspire us? How do we do more of that type of work?

Do Bonuses Increase Engagement? (If Not, What Does?)

A fascinating and talented leader, Neil, asked that question. Then he provided the evidence that, in fact, bonuses *do not* increase engagement.

The organization Neil works for completed an engagement survey during a period when they hadn't paid any bonuses (for the first time ever). The results showed that engagement was down. Neil reported many people said, "I am not surprised by the poor scores . . . we haven't paid bonuses. Next year we'll pay a big bonus . . . and the engagement data will soar."

"Guess what?" Neil said. "The next year we paid one of the biggest bonuses in years. And the engagement score hardly moved at all. This goes to prove:

You can't fix an intangible problem with a tangible solution."

Leaders who are activators, who can quickly develop the performance capability in others, know the difference between tangible solutions and the intangible.

Neil explained: "It happens all the time: People complain, 'They don't communicate with me!' Yet, these same people get hundreds of emails a day, e-bulletins from every department, and are invited to more meetings than they can attend. What people are really saying is, 'I am not *included.*'" (There's a distinction between communicating at someone and including that person.)

"People are asking for intangible solutions," Neil said. "But what most companies are doing to increase engagement is responding with tangible solutions. But intangible needs and tangible solutions are two different things."

I work for pay. But there's something else I'm after. And when you help me get it, you get more of me.

Long Lever Questions:

1. Currently, what are employees agitated (complaining) about – and what are the intangible solutions they are really asking for?

2. What does it look like for us to be more aware of the intangible-solution response in our daily interactions?

3. As members of this team, what are the intangible solutions we've received that we most value? And why?

For videos and resources to support engagement, visit
http://oneteambook.com/engagement

How to Amplify Excellence

Try this experiment: Identify a child you know well, mark your calendar, and during the coming year only give that child feedback once. Then, assess the child's behavior development.

Got any predictions? (Agreed: The child's behavior would likely get ugly.)

Even though the fundamentals of an adult's brain are consistent with those of a child's, some workplaces replicate the mock experiment stated above. Consequently, they are dead zones for feedback.

Got any predictions on the performance development of these employees?

Relentless adaptability is the new "must" in business. An effective team has members running parallel to one another, anticipating, responding, correcting, and adapting to the changes and actions around them. Feedback is the primary and necessary mechanism for growing the capability of agility.

Equally important is the type of feedback provided. **A team cannot say they are devoted to excellence if they're dedicated to focusing primarily on failures.**
(The exception is a "learning failure" that proves to be a tremendous resource.) The two are not compatible. You go toward your focus; therefore, you get more of what you focus on.

This can be a challenge for high performers. You have succeeded by eliminating flaws, gaps, and errors. You zero in on mistakes like birds of prey intent to kill. Yet, if you could only choose one, which would you select: a team that thoroughly understands why it's failing or a team that has confidence and comprehends what's necessary for success? The distinction between these two is a differentiator.

In the pursuit of excellence, eliminating poor performance remains a slower method than developing high performance. When the greater percentage of feedback happens during moments of healthy risk taking, learning, and success, you can expect to win more.

The choice is yours. What will you amplify with your feedback: Poor performance – or excellence?

Long Lever Questions:

1. Do we reserve feedback largely as a "top-down" device – or are we also providing feedback to peers as well?

2. What are the characteristics of a person who receives and uses feedback well?

3. When we do give feedback, which do we do most: Acknowledge a task well done – or the demonstration of a shared value or behavior? (What would be the benefit if we did more of the latter?)

The Loser Syndrome And Its Cost

For years I suffered "Minnesota Viking Syndrome." (I assure you: It's painful.)

Growing up in the northern portion of the U.S., I adopted the local professional (American) football team, the Vikings, as my favorite. Each year, every season, always held promise. And occasionally the team prevailed – almost.

Four times the Minnesota Vikings have fought their way to the biggest, final game: the Super Bowl. And four times they've lost.

We're losers. As of the publication of this piece, not once have the Vikings walked off the field with the trophy in hand. And so, as a fan, celebrations are as rare as sighting comets.

Do you know work teams who never celebrate until they win the big one? They wait until the end of the quarter or the conclusion of the project to determine if they're winners. And, if there is any evidence they missed perfection, that they didn't win, then they determine by default that they are – you guessed it – losers.

If high performance is always a finish line we haven't crossed, then we remain losers. Equally important, if success is only defined as beating the competition, then we're at risk of devoting our focus to variables outside our control. (And the champagne is kept on ice.)

Believing we are winners must be learned *before* the results of the title game are in hand, before the project is finished. This thinking reinforces a focus that improves results: We now *expect* to function at our potential.

Excellence is not an outcome, but a spirit and confidence we breathe into every action and conversation.

Teams that selectively celebrate the seemingly small milestones and unheralded acts of excellence have an advantage: They create more achievement.

The acknowledgement, the celebration – even in the form of a thank you or a handwritten note – establishes the wisdom that losing is something that may happen to us. But it is not who we are.

Long Lever Questions:

1. Does our team believe we are winners? And what's the significance of our answer?

2. How would you assess our "aptitude for celebration"?

3. What are effective ways to celebrate that are inclusive (team oriented, rather than highlighting the individual) and will drive more of the behaviors we want to see?

Bonus: Where do we have momentum in our business now that's worthy of a celebration?

Don't Apologize

The old thinking and approach to teamwork still stains some workplaces like the smell of beer that won't leave an abused college apartment. Without a cleaning crew, business suffers.

A leader who thinks like you do, who knows that culture eats strategy for breakfast, told us something that reminds team-oriented leaders their mission is not complete. He was on a conference call with "one of the most difficult-to-work-for leaders in the organization. Yet, things were actually improving" between this leader's team and others in the organization.

At the end of the call, the leader revealed her view of and approach to teamwork: "I'm feeling sappy today," she said. "So I'll tell you that I feel like we're turning the corner on the trust between our teams."

Feeling sappy?

What's sappy about trust? What's silly about being purposeful in developing the one-team competencies and culture necessary for success? What's foolish about acknowledging or expressing gratitude for the necessary ingredient to succeed together?

The outdated stench that trust and other behaviors are defined as "fluffy" or "sappy" still permeates. What does this mean for those of us who know that how we work together is a primary variable for increasing high performance?

We still have work to do.

Don't apologize for your passion and determination for finishing the job of building one team.

Be seen today. Be heard today. Ask the question today. Listen today. Activate inspired teamwork.

Long Lever Questions:

1. Where does trust stand as a priority for us? And is our answer consistent with our daily interactions?

2. Are there forces within our organization that discount cultural components such as trust? And if so, what does it look like for us to "be seen and heard today"?

3. What's the benefit to us for being bold in our actions to build one-team behaviors such as trust throughout our organization?

Big Ideas That Provide The Fulcrum Of Wisdom For Your Long Lever Questions

Activation Point: Pride

When we belong to something bigger than who we are as individuals we are called to do more. Pride – the sort that goes beyond self – is priceless. When this occurs the members of a collective endeavor get something back in return for their efforts that can't be purchased with money.

Activation Point: Growth

Most organizations have a DNA formed from generations doing business where there was only one leader per team. Now, developing leadership, talent, and team have an equal share of the spotlight and become a priority for every business. This is calling us to be effective at fulfilling our potential as people.

Activation Point: Partnerships

High-performing teams develop effective partnerships at and beyond the traditional boundaries of their team, thereby expanding the border of their influence. They seize seemingly mundane interactions to create the conditions that form and nurture strong *relationships*.

Activation Point: Excellence

Believing you don't have what's necessary to succeed means you're choosing to fail. Excellence isn't an outcome, it's an action. The solutions to the problems we've never seen before begin to reveal themselves as we become better at being who we believe we can be.

Activation Point: Proactive

The length of time a team waits to be told what to do is in direct proportion to an organization's profitability. Four categories of co-discover questions – Alignment-to-Objectives or Vision, Execution, Motivation, and Accountability – facilitate the thinking that influence proactive performance.

Activation Point: Diversity

Great teams are composed of people who spend little time minimizing teammates. Together, they ask for – in fact, they insist on – people being the truest expression of who they are. They don't require people to be less; they ask for more in a way that delivers the mission of the team.

Activation Point: Inspiration

A team achieves excellence when they're inspired by the notion of experiencing it. The human spirit was not meant to conform. Inspired self-expression, both individually and as a team, brings with it a boldness that smashes through the productivity levels of the compliant workplace.

Activation Point: Engagement

People are asking for intangible solutions. But what most companies are doing to increase engagement is responding with tangible solutions. But intangible needs and tangible solutions are two different things. When the intangible need is met, teammates give more.

Activation Point: Feedback

In the pursuit of excellence, eliminating poor performance remains a slower method than developing high performance. When the greater percentage of feedback happens during moments of healthy risk taking, learning, and success, you can expect to win more.

Activation Point: Celebration

Believing we are winners must be learned before results are in, before the project is finished. This paradigm reinforces a focus that improves results: We now *expect* to function at our potential. Excellence is not an outcome, but a spirit and confidence we breathe into every action and conversation.

Activation Point: Trust

The outdated stench that trust and other behaviors be defined as "fluffy" or "sappy" still permeates workplaces. Don't apologize for your passion and determination for finishing the job of building one team. Be seen today. Be heard today. Ask the question today. Listen today. Activate inspired teamwork.

Download a quick reference of all chapter summaries at
http://oneteambook.com/chaptersummaries

ONE TEAM PROGRESS ASSESSMENT

Congratulations: You've worked your plan of leveraging 52 Activation Points to develop the one-team behavioral competencies essential to elevating the High Performance Ceiling. Before answering the assessment questions below, review your notes from previous discussions. Then, compare where your team was a year ago with the strength you're demonstrating today.

A. At the start of this book we identified what success would look like as we developed a greater "one-team" approach. *To what extent – and how – did we meet our expectations?*

B. *Where did we miss on our expectations – and what did we learn in those areas?*

C. *Where did we exceed our objectives?*

D. *Which Activation Points have proven to be most important to discuss and why?* We challenge you to identify the "Top 10" so you can return to these in the future, assess your progress, and further activate the potential that exists.

E. *Are there any Activation Points and Long Lever Questions we should revisit and further discuss now?* As any team develops they discover challenges that require the development of new behavioral competencies. Perhaps your team read something together weeks ago that wasn't as relevant as it will be today.

F. *What commitments and actionable plan can we create to sustain our momentum in strengthening inspired teamwork?*

Successes from the Field

Driving Greater Levels Of Responsibility In The Team

As if succeeding in business isn't challenging enough, imagine this scenario: You've made the sale – the customer wants your product – and then you discover your organization can't fulfill the orders. What do you do? Consider that any sarcastic thoughts that may enter your head actually shape the actions of some leaders. Companies everywhere are filled with legendary tales of bosses transforming into tyrants in similar scenarios.

If you're Alison (a leader with inspired vision) though, you rise to the occasion: In the midst of a crisis you not only rely on your team – you strengthen it. Long Lever Questions is how that is done.

"The fill rate on one of our most important products is currently just over 50 percent," Alison said. "It's a significant hit, and one we saw coming.

Whether we like the data or not, it's a priority for me that the team not be a victim to the circumstances.

We must have team members taking full responsibility in their roles as we work our plan."

This is no time for cheerleading. No time for emotional demands that shake the confidence of the team to deliver. It is time to activate inspired teamwork.

The Long Lever Question Alison used blended the reality of the situation – along with the behaviors she knew she had to see. (Note the important distinction: She resisted the temptation of telling people what to do, and instead focus on who they had to *be*.)

First, she set the question up for success by stating the reality of the severe situation: "Here's the data. Here's where we stand." Next, she informed her team what must happen and why: "We must take full responsibility and act swiftly in our roles to ensure we deliver on our customer-centric values."

Then, Alison asked her Long Lever Question: "Given the data and other input we're getting, how will we demonstrate the responsibility individually and collectively that is necessary to win as we work through this issue?"

This is a strong Long Lever Question for many reasons, including the fact that it connects an expectation to an inherent personal motivation that resides inside most of us: We want to show that our character is strong. We want to reveal our greatness. As a leader, Alison understands this fundamental need and doesn't just invite her team to respond accordingly – she expects it.

Alison reported to us, "I then came back to this theme and their responses throughout the meeting. It provided the perfect structure I needed to have confidence we could overcome the obstacle."

While most of the case studies in this book clearly demonstrate the effect Long Lever Questions have on business performance, the story above is a work in progress. The interview was conducted as final drafts of this book were being prepared. It is with high confidence that we included it, however, as Alison and her team have a track record of success with the

One Team approach: They've led their organization to double-digit growth the last three-plus years.

Because Alison consistently activates the greatness in her team, it's likely this year will be an extension of the trend in excellence that already exists.

Developing The Skill Of Using
Long Lever Questions

3 Techniques For Developing The Skill:
Technique #1: Finish The Question
Technique #2: Focus On Values Over Tasks
Technique #3: Point At The Specific Issue

When poor results or outcomes are realized, some people choose to fume, rant, pontificate, or "vent." Such approaches may satisfy their need to be authentic and transparent with teammates, yet these tactics fall short in improving performance They only create incremental progress forward – at best.

What's needed is someone willing to step up, speak out, and take action that influences the future. And nothing moves people collectively forward like Long Lever Questions. In these situations, the technique of pointing directly at the specific issue creates the context necessary to give any question more leverage.

Here's an example of what that looks like: "With the one-week window we have, **what's next** to improve performance in a manner the customer wishes to see?"

You'd never know it, but consider that the teammate who's asking this question is deeply concerned about the shrinking window of time facing the team before their deadline arrives. Of course, it makes perfect sense in situations like this for the inquirer to use a platform statement prior to asking the question, such as "I'm deeply concerned that we're running out of time." Because we always go toward our focus, what we're focused on becomes significantly important. Team members, especially those with strong levels of influential power, are cautioned to be sparing in expressing their anxieties and worries. **Who wants to work for or with someone who's regularly communicating or "venting" frustration, concerns, or fears?** It's not inspiring, and usually diverts people to minimalist thinking and actions.

These are the situations where the third technique for crafting Long Lever Questions is particularly useful. Pointing at the specific issue in the questions allows the inquirer to be direct and provide the clarity necessary to drive increased accountability. Here are five key words and phrases that can be used to begin Long Lever Questions that point at specific issues:

1. Given

2. Because

3. Due to

4. Regarding

5. As a result of

Shown here are examples of what those queries might look like. Additionally, for contrast, the common short-lever questions are listed first in *italics*.

Short-lever question :
How will we improve?

LONG LEVER QUESTION:
Given the team didn't hit the deadline, what's the essential lesson we need to carry forward to ensure success in similar situations?

Short-lever question:
What are we going to do now?

LONG LEVER QUESTION:
Because of the news we just received, why is it important to this team that we respond in a way that's consistent with our stated values?

Short-lever question:
What's important here?

LONG LEVER QUESTION:
Due to the pending reorganization, what's the most important work that we should focus on now that is critical to the business?

Short-lever question:
What do we need to talk about?

LONG LEVER QUESTION:
Regarding the rumors that are swirling around here, what are our responsibilities in terms of how we communicate and interact with one another?

Short-lever question:
What can we do about this?

LONG LEVER QUESTION:
As a result of this unfortunate news, how do we want to respond and create the best outcome possible?

Pointing at the issue is usually most effective when done at the beginning of the question. This leaves the trigger portion of the question, which activates the focus and potential you're seeking, for the end. Ultimately, though, there are no "Long-Lever-Question Police" roaming out there, so most importantly: begin.

A Leader In Trouble

Lance was in trouble. He had been given the responsibility to lead a department where most of the employees had 15-plus-years of experience in the focused area – yet he had little expertise in this aspect of the business.

He devoured the idea of asking Long Lever Questions, because he saw it as his method for leveraging the wisdom and experience of those he was responsible for leading. Diligently he practiced the three techniques to constructing effective Long Lever Questions:

1. Technique #1: Finish The Question

2. Technique #2: Focus On Values Over Tasks

3. Technique #3: Point At The Specific Issue

Success rarely comes in a flash, however. During the sustainability phase of our training, Lance shared that the performance in the department had plateaued. And the feedback he was getting on his leadership wasn't what he'd hoped for: The team was reporting confusion, vaguely defined roles, lack of direction and accountability.

"Do Long Lever Questions really work?" Lance wondered. Having observed Lance in action with his team, we knew there was a better question he could ask himself. Research on the brain, thinking, and social dynamics – along with the experience of thousands of leaders before him – prove the effectiveness of Long Lever Questions. Therefore, the better question for Lance to ask is: How do I make my Long Lever Questions more effective?

Platform Statements: Give Your Question A Foundation

To help Lance more clearly understand the importance of asking Long Lever Questions, I sat next to him and placed a medium-sized book on the table. Then I grabbed a plastic measuring stick about 30 centimeters long, held it up, and said, "This is your lever." Next, I took a small, square stone from Lance's desk that had been fashioned for use as a paperweight and said, "This is your fulcrum."

There was, however, an important detail to add. Grabbing what I could reach, I placed disheveled papers, a few pens, Lance's smartphone, and a portion of an uneaten bagel in a pile. Upon this mess I placed the paperweight (fulcrum).

The results were predictable: Each time Lance attempted to move (or influence) the book by use of the lever, the fulcrum (paperweight) slid off the unstable clutter, leaving the lever virtually useless. At this point, Lance became annoyed and brushed aside the papers, pens, and bagel, emphatically placed the paperweight (fulcrum) firmly on the table, then used his lever to lift the book into the air.

The metaphor was complete. Earlier in the day we had observed Lance, with the best of intentions, asking Long Lever Questions. He was doing so, however, with little or no explanation to his team about what he was attempting to achieve with such inquiries. From the looks on their faces, members of his team were confused.

A typical day for anyone on Lance's team involved multiple priorities, processing significant and complex data, and mounting pressures to improve performance. Asking Long Lever Questions without explanation is akin to setting a fulcrum on chaos or "clutter." To be more successful, Lance didn't need to change the words in his Long Lever Questions; he needed to establish a platform, a solid foundation, for his questions to reveal their power.

What A Platform Statement Sounds Like

Platform Statements have three primary purposes:

1. They provide the context or purpose for asking the Long Lever Question. An example: "I'm sensing we need greater alignment before we end this meeting." (Long Lever Question follows.)

2. They acknowledge or validate the perspective or feelings of others. An example: "I know you are frustrated with the ban on travel and other resource limitations." (Long Lever Question follows.)

3. They provide the means to communicate your perspectives, feelings, or expectations. An example: "I'm proud of the way you engaged in vigorous debate with the customer in such a way that exposed some flaws we must remedy in our approach." (Long Lever Question follows.)

Lance's team reported confusion, vaguely defined roles, lack of direction and accountability. One could assume that these outcomes were due to Lance's inexperience in his new field of responsibility. While that could certainly be a variable, we must ask: Why is it that some people can go into areas of business where they have little experience and still successfully influence or lead the team forward?

Time and again, we see evidence that success in these situations is a function of the person's ability to use in combination clarifying Platform Statements and tailored Long Lever Questions. In other words,

Lance didn't need to be a technical expert: He needed to develop his leadership expertise.

After our coaching, here are examples of what Lance used as Platform Statements, along with the Long Lever Questions he asked:

1. <u>Platform Statement</u>: "It's imperative that we have clarity in our objectives so that we can better define our next action steps. Therefore, I want to better understand your perspectives."

   a. <u>Long Lever Question</u>: "What is the definition of success our internal customer is communicating to us, both in the projects we've completed and in those we're currently working on?"

2. <u>Platform Statement</u>: "We must ensure our individual roles on this project are clearly defined to ensure the greatest efficiencies. And because I want you to take ownership of your responsibilities, I'm going to ask us all to respond to this question."

   a. <u>Long Lever Question</u>: "What do you see as your specific contribution to this project, that you will be accountable for delivering and therefore drive our team's success?"

3. <u>Platform Statement</u>: "It's essential that we each step up and speak out when we have information that is critical to the team's success. This also includes those incidences when we don't feel we have the clarity or information we need to be accountable to our responsibilities."

   a. <u>Long Lever Question</u>: "Who on this team models the ability to step up and seek clarity and information – and do so in a way that generates stronger team performance?"

Mind Readers Are In Demand

Lance confessed that while he had shown greater capability in asking powerful questions, it was his opinion that his new team was not accustomed to being asked to think. Plus, he had "assumed" those around him could read his mind on *why* he was asking the questions. That, however, was not a skill for which the organization had been hiring.

Therefore, Lance made the commitment to "thinking out loud" and being transparent about the reasons why he was asking questions.

We've supported Lance over the year since the coaching above occurred. As this book went to press, Lance was reviewing the 360 degree survey his organization recently conducted to provide him unfiltered feedback from those around him. Gone are the comments of confusion, lack of clarity, and issues surrounding accountability. Instead, the report reveals aptitudes associated with decisiveness and direction. And a business performing at higher levels.

Create A New Normal

While in high school I had the opportunity to have a private basketball lesson with one of the top coaches in the state. Things were going well until he said, "Okay. Now let's see you go to the basket using your left hand."

I swallowed hard. I'm right-handed. Showing him the lack of skill I had in using my opposite hand wouldn't be fun. With methodical and careful moves, I dribbled toward the basket, left the floor, and put the ball up with my left hand. Thankfully, it went through the basket.

After retrieving the ball, the coach stood in front of me and asked, "Did that feel awkward?"

I couldn't lie. "Yes ."

"You need to know that it looked completely normal," he said.

"Really?" I was surprised by his assessment.

"Really," he answered. Then he finished with something that both inspired and scared me. "You need to quit worrying about how you look, and worry more about how you contribute. Until you develop the skills in your opposite hand, you're half the player you can be. And that means you're robbing your team of half your ability to help them win games."

The idea of robbing my team of wins was sobering – and has inspired me to continually stretch myself with a continuous-improvement mindset. As I grew older, I discovered that there were other people – many others – who are dedicated to mastering their chosen craft. The results they've achieved by learning how to contribute more have changed the world we all live in.

Asking Long Lever Questions may feel and sound awkward at first. It could be perceived as clunky, and not "culturally normal." Use this unease to your advantage: It's a sign that you're on the verge of expanding your repertoire to more effectively influence others, of ensuring those you're devoted to serving are not robbed of your greatest potential.

Besides, a team committed to doing only what's normal or looks good is committed to the status quo.

Stepping up, speaking out, and leading in ways that stretch thinking and actions are required to consistently raise the High Performance Ceiling. To make this happen, we challenge you to use the techniques listed above and ask one Long Lever Question a week. This can be pre-scripted, if you like. Then, as you gain more confidence and apply what you're learning, the challenge becomes to ask one Long Lever Question per day.

The opportunity lies in creating a new normal. Somewhere near you a team with tremendous potential waits to be inspired.

CHAPTER NINE

What We Are Capable Of Achieving Together

What Sort Of Influence Will You Apply?

What your team is talking about is where your team is going. To change any discussion, you must apply influence. It's in this moment, as you choose the type of stimulus you'll apply, that you can differentiate yourself as a team member and elevate your team's performance.

Many people succumb to applying a force that is so grossly overused, it's blunted to the point of being nearly powerless: They tell and tell and tell people what to do or what others should think. *ONE Team* delivers a proven alternative. Long Lever Questions provide inspired team members with the power needed to change conversations, develop and amplify wisdom, and activate inspired teamwork.

Predict Discoveries For Your Team

Karen is a middle manager who expressed a fear to us: "I'm afraid if I ask questions my team will go places I can't predict or that I don't want them to go." After acknowledging her candor, we got a chance to watch her in action, and quickly saw the potential she possessed to influence her team in significantly greater ways.

Karen's team spent excessive amounts of time in meetings having discussions that were far from productive. The dialogue often meandered aimlessly. Sometimes several team members would become trapped in "swirls" where unseen forces sucked them into repetitive discourse and pointless analysis and the objectives became lost.

The irony was obvious: Karen's fear of asking the team questions and taking them to places she couldn't define was subjecting them to certain dysfunction – and a speed that would not allow them to be competitive. Because Karen was smart enough to see the arrested progress of her team, she did what we see most people in similar situations default to doing: She talked at her team even more. More directions. More commands. More spelling everything out for them. Slowly, and surely, she was programming them to be only followers, to be non-thinkers waiting for their daily dose of directives.

With their daily grind only delivering mediocre results, Karen confessed that she was becoming increasingly cynical of the idea that anything about her job could be inspiring.

After we coached her on the control issues – which were perpetuating a low performance ceiling – we introduced the skill of asking Long Lever Questions. One of the first Long Lever Questions Karen asked her teammates was this: "What will we commit to achieving this week that's important to our customer?"

The change that occurred – the activation of potential within the team – occurred within minutes.

In time, she increasingly experienced what you and your team have had reinforced through the 52 Activation Points in *ONE Team*: The more consistently she used her influence to elevate the thinking of those around her, the more it resulted in a change of dialogue. Because the team altered what they were talking about, they changed what they were doing. And their High Performance Ceiling began to rise.

As Karen practiced Long Lever Questions she realized that her fear of being unable to predict where her team would go was unfounded. In fact, the opposite was true: With enhanced specificity she was able to leverage their collective focus in pinpoint fashion – not to wisdom she already had, but far beyond to discoveries she and the team made together.

Look Up

Imagine you'd saved money for the vacation of a lifetime: a visit to the

Sistine Chapel. You arrive in Vatican City, approach the storied structure, and walk in – yet during the visit you never look up. Instead, your gaze sits at eye level. Upon leaving, you miss what many claim is the most breathtaking sight a human can see: Michelangelo's painting of "The Last Judgment" on the chapel's ceiling, a work that forever changed western art.

Or maybe you journey to the Grand Canyon in the western United States. Yet, once at the edge of the awe-inspiring vista where you can witness billions of years of natural forces at play, you choose only to read about the canyon in the park guide.

Or maybe it's the championship game of the World Cup football tournament you travel to see, only to stay in the parking lot and listen to the crowd in the coliseum beyond.

Such near misses with the inspired and spectacular are travesties. It seems ludicrous: Who would invest such efforts, travel so far and so closely to greatness, and not choose to seize such tremendous opportunities?

The answer, unfortunately, is that millions make this choice every day.

People travel far over the course of their careers only to miss what is always oh so close and available to them in a moment.

A. The teams they are a part of are only called that by name. In reality, they are only groups of people who move through a get-the-work-done grind with their heads down and vision obscured.

B. Inspiration is only experienced when they think about the weekend or retirement.

C. Days pass, another reorganization happens, their job is miraculously spared, and they find themselves grouped with different people who are as anxious as they are.

D. In time, some give up (they just don't tell their boss). Other people get angry and express it in unproductive ways. Still others leave, and jump from one employer to the next, searching for a company or leader somewhere "who understands."

Yet, thousands of times over, in these situations and more, the evidence shows that all which is required for a team to see more, to be and do more, is one person to look up – and ask a Long Lever Question.

Author Kathryn Schulz brilliantly stated, "The miracle of your mind isn't that you can see the world as it is. It's that you can see the world as it isn't."[1] Strategically focused curiosity – achieved by asking Long Lever Questions – enables your team to see a more significant vision. What is it you're eager for the team you're on to know about themselves that isn't yet known? Where will the team discover they can go that they have yet to consider?

Long Lever Questions activate inspired teamwork because they elevate thinking while connecting people to a purpose that reminds everyone: This is why I'm here. **This is why I've traveled so far with my teammates. This is what we are capable of achieving together.**

Change The Discussion The World Is Having
Our world is changing. What sort of change occurs will be determined by those who choose to participate. Where will we go together? As members of the largest team – the human race – we don't need more people telling us what to do and what we should think. We need greater participation.

We need more people activating inspired teamwork.

It's time to change from a culture dominated by individuals talking at people to one where we are talking with one another. History proves that when we have such inspired discussions at local levels we transform what we're capable of accomplishing together at national and international levels.

You are now further equipped to rearrange thinking and inspire others to act differently. This is but one step we want to take with you. We'd like to join you in your quest to strengthen teams everywhere, and ask that you enable the book you're holding to leverage the wisdom of others: Pass it along. Hand these pages to people you know who want to use their influence for an outcome that goes far beyond anything they could achieve individually.

As more people ask Long Lever Questions, the discussions in our homes, businesses and communities, and our world will increasingly transform actions in inspiring ways. This shift reinforces what we all know to be true: We can deliver on our greater purpose.

Give me a lever long enough ... and I can move the world.

What will you move today that's important to you?

APPENDIX A | **BONUS MATERIAL**

Only For Teams With Guts

This is a true story. (That had to be stated; there are some who don't believe what follows is possible.)

Jill is not normal. Specifically, she refuses to be victim to anyone's leadership deficiencies, especially those above her on the organizational chart.

Employees working for chronically backward-focused "higher-ups" in the organization often become backward focused themselves. (We've likely all been there.) There are some people, however, who demonstrate an ability to be autonomous of any boss's ineptitude; they go about their productive day unscathed.

Jill is one such person. "I'm amazed at how well this has worked," she said. "By staying true to my values, including having my boss's back even when I disagree with his approach, more change has been created than I thought possible."

What started as an individual quest transformed into team determination. "In the past, everyone on the team would consistently see the worst of him (the boss). Now we increasingly focus on the best in him. The result is our boss is gradually getting better as a leader."

Jill and the team she's on didn't create change simply by *seeing* their boss differently; their ability to manage what they can control resulted in *leading* their boss differently.

Being a victim requires minimal effort. It can seem safer to surrender and say, "Screw this." It takes a team with guts to lead with integrity, to treat a boss how we would like that person to lead us. Doing so, especially when there's no guarantee those above us will change, is the excellence of self.

As a high performer, it's doubtful you function from your values for the sake of changing others. There are, after all, motivations far more grand.

1. To what extent is our level of effort contingent on the actions of others?

2. What motivates us to relentlessly give our best, regardless of the circumstances around us?

3. What does it look like to "have someone's back" even when we disagree with that person's approach?

When PTO = *Pretend* Time Off

"Joe, I really hope you enjoy your vacation with your family," the boss said as Joe walked out the door. Two days later, as Joe was fishing with his children, he received his fifteenth text message from his boss screaming for an answer.

Joe's kids wondered: "This is a vacation?"

Bottom line: Employees don't unplug unless the leaders around them unplug.

The pressures of business can distort definitions. PTO is supposed to mean Paid Time Off. As in, the employee is *not* working. Some teams, though, create an environment where being a team player means you're available 24/7. They interpret PTO to mean *Pretend* Time Off. In these cases when an employee says, "I'm on vacation," others hear "I'm working outside the office."

Sustained excellence in business is a function of discipline in both mental and physical health. As a team it's worth getting aligned on what's necessary for excellence as it relates to personal health. Consider:

1. The price of PTO should be effective collaboration. Any person's PTO is a *team* effort. Rather than making it the employee's sole responsibility to avoid emails or phone calls while he's with family, successful teams fight for their peer's health by limiting communications.

2. There are those who make little distinction between their work and play.[1] Occasionally, what you're after is not time away from your passion (others may call it work), but an

alternative structure, pace, or environment. (Beach sand can be inspiring.) If you're going to work while you're away, set communications expectations with your team. For example, 30 minutes per day of connection while on PTO, and only respond to critical matters.

3. And for those who believe they can't stop working, lest they fall short of their potential: "Rest" is part of our job. Downtime is critical to sustained excellence. This means that time away from the office is actually important *work*. In the big picture, investing in ourselves by turning off our smartphone is a strategy to becoming an even higher performer.

Long Lever Questions:

1. How is PTO defined and valued by our team? And what do we want it to mean?

2. What opportunities do we have to ensure that the investment of any PTO is fully maximized?

3. What's the specific payoff to our team as we effectively execute one person's PTO?

For videos and resources to support you in your personal life, visit
http://oneteambook.com/personal

What You Can't See Can Limit You

It may be what we can't see that limits our ability to *be*. Some of our limits are invisible. But we can feel them.

Flying into Mexico City is an experience. From above, you can see a patchwork of roads and buildings that looks like a complex jigsaw puzzle. Once on the ground, you enjoy the vibrant culture and remarkable people, oblivious to the macro transportation challenge facing the city. But once in a car you quickly detect the predicament: Driving across the metropolis can take all day.

While patterns of poor results may be caused by our own fatigue or incapable colleagues, there is another variable that may be causing unsatisfactory results: inadequate or misaligned systems and structures. In other words, it's not us or them who are the cause – but it.

These silent and seemingly indiscernible forces, when left unattended, create friction and confusion: When do we do what? Where? How? And with whom?

Even the mightiest "A" player will be under pressure to disengage under the weight of misaligned or flawed systems. By acknowledging the forces, by observing and talking about them, we create the opportunity to shape and evolve those systems so we can work more effectively together and break through the High Performance Ceiling.

High performers are like water: given the opportunity, they will find the most direct course to delivering the objective.

Today the terrain changes often. When this happens, and teams are unaware of the influence of systems or structure, the water may suddenly pool and stand.

What's your next move?

Long Lever Questions:

1. What are some signs that we have a system or structure issue (rather than a personnel challenge)?

2. What does it look like to be more purposeful in the understanding and development of our systems?

3. What expectations do we have for ourselves as a team if we find ourselves in a system or structure we perceive is inadequate but can't change immediately?

The Habits of Excellence

Have you been with that certain someone in a car when, turning a corner, you discover you're in a traffic jam? The response is sometimes curious: Shouts of frustrations, sighs of dismay, even physical stress is displayed as they become victims to their circumstances.

Sometimes this disabling habit is so ingrained that all people need to do is *hear* about a traffic jam on the radio and they succumb to agony.

Behavior repeated consistently becomes a habit. This is true for the individual and the collective. Therefore, are the behaviors we're consistently demonstrating as a team harmful or helpful habits?

As a team, how do we respond when:

1. A customer challenges us?

2. Another team refuses to collaborate with us?

3. We make a mistake?

4. We perceive we don't have the resources we need?

5. Others impose demands on us?

Teams that consistently elevate their High Performance Ceiling start their meetings on time, use agendas, use decision-making structures, and openly communicate not just when in crisis. These behaviors were established as habits long before "bad news" arrived.

Destructive habits chart a course for dysfunction. Conversely, consistency of targeted behaviors brings increasing confidence we're moving toward our chosen goal. Developing the discipline of consistency brings a sort of control that liberates teams even in their most challenging moments. Teams that function as one are bigger than the obstacles they encounter, not because they possess helicopters to fly over traffic jams, but because they are consistent with high-performance behaviors long before issues ever occur.

Long Lever Questions:

1. What habits might we have now that are not productive and which we should move past?

2. When challenges appear, what might be indicators that we're using outdated patterns of responses?

3. Collectively, what behaviors do we want to model more consistently in response to issues?

Bonus: What are our specific motivations for creating new team habits of excellence?

"Judge a man by his questions rather than by his answers."

- Voltaire

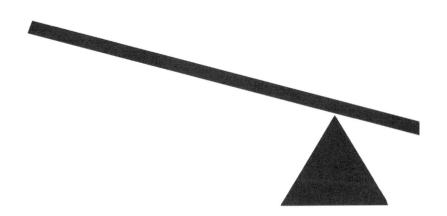

APPENDIX B | **LONG LEVER QUESTIONS FEEDBACK FORM**

Long Lever Questions Feedback Form

Ask a team member to observe you in a meeting and use this form for feedback.

Name_____

Meeting _____ Date_____

_____ # of Long Lever Questions asked.

Examples of questions asked:

_____

_____

_____

_____ # of short-lever questions asked.

_____

_____

1. Ratio of time used talking/telling/directing – in relation to time spent asking questions/listening. (Example: 60% - 40%)

   _____ % of time spent talking/telling/directing

   _____ % of time asking questions/listening

2. Strengths in meeting leadership, particularly actions that developed and supported a "one-team" approach.

   _____

   _____

   _____

3. Improvement opportunities to ask more effective questions.

   _____

   _____

   _____

Template available at http://oneteambook.com/feedbackform |

ACKNOWLEDGMENTS

It's really quite simple: There's nothing like being on an inspired team, both in the results that are created and the experience one gains. As authors, we are fortunate to be a part of what we believe is the world's greatest team. The members of this team are not confined to those who receive their paycheck from the same source. The team we're talking about here expands far beyond traditional boundaries, to include our customers, a remarkable network of support people, friends, and family members. All of you make our lives richer, and remind us that the process of discovery is as valuable as the achievement of our goals.

First, a significant debt of gratitude is owed to those individuals – those inspired leaders – we call client-partners. It's your determination to build great teams and high-performing workplaces that compels us to bring forth an even greater effort each day. You know who you are, because we identify you as friends. We relish our interactions with you, and enjoy every celebration we have together as you achieve your goals.

We want to especially thank those client-partners and friends who willingly invested their important time to review various drafts of this book. Your feedback assured the quality we were determined to deliver. Your selfless act has been generous and is greatly appreciated.

To our teammates at Verus Global . . . we can't stand tall enough in our applause. Talk about one team! Each of you teach and inspire us in ways you can't imagine. Our gratitude for your passion, focus, and tireless efforts is immeasurable.

Specifically, as it relates to the effort behind *ONE Team,* we'd like to thank Theresa Letman; your diligence and determination never ceases to amaze us. Lisa Marie Main, how do you do it all? Your understanding of how "it" all fits together, along with your knowledge of the human spirit, is something we couldn't do without. Sherilyn Jayne, your research and "lets-do-it-all" attitude refreshes us more often than you know. And without a doubt, we know this book would have never materialized had it not been for the focus and follow-through of these team members: Denise Pushnik, Lisa Teets, Steve Drury, Celes Deering, Sandy Vanlerberghe, Beverly Jones, Cindy Main, Bob Burgess, Tyler Anderson, Steve Vannoy, Brett Kleffner, Sue Taigman, Sheryl Alstrin, Peter Stolze, Pilar Pardo, Brenda Trejos, Kevin Gray, and Victor McGuire. Thank you all for teaming with us to bring *ONE Team* to the world.

Doug Reeves, you're more than a book coach: You're a friend who sees and activates the brilliance and potential in others. Your wisdom repeatedly proves valuable.

We consider our editor, Ruth Goodman, one of the finest in the industry. "All in" in every way, we thank you for your skill, agility, and professionalism you bring to our team.

Last, and in so many ways most importantly, we'd like to thank our respective families. Without your support and unconditional love we know such books as the one you're holding now would remain an "idea." Thank you for allowing us to disappear, find our way home long after the lights are out, and seek greater truths even in those moments when you just want to discuss what's for dinner.

We have felt your love each step of the way, and are eternally grateful for how you activate our inspired efforts.

BIBLIOGRAPHY & NOTES

OPENING
1. Multiple sources.

PROLOGUE
1. Berra, Yogi, and Dave Kaplan. *You Can Observe a Lot by Watching: What I've Learned About Teamwork from the Yankees and Life.* Hoboken, NJ: John Wiley & Sons, 2008.
2. Tuckman, Bruce W. "Developmental sequence in small groups." *Psychological Bulletin* 63, no. 6 (1965): 384-99. doi:10.1037/h0022100.
3. Bennis, Warren. *Managing People Is Like Herding Cats: On Leadership.* Provo, UT: Executive Excellence Pub., 1999.

CHAPTER 1
1. Kiley, David. "The New Heat On Ford." *Bloomberg Businessweek,* June 03, 2007. http://www.businessweek.com/stories/2007-06-03/the-new-heat-on-ford.
2. Caldicott, Sarah Miller. "Why Alan Mulally Is An Innovation CEO For The Record Books." *Forbes,* June 25, 2014. http://www.forbes.com/sites/sarahcaldicott/2014/06/25/why-fords-alan-mulally-is-an-innovation-ceo-for-the-record-books/.
3. "Leading in the 21st century: An interview with Ford's Alan Mulally." *McKinsey & Company,* November 2013. http://www.mckinsey.com/insights/strategy/leading_in_the_21st_century_an_interview_with_fords_alan_mulally.
4. Kiley, David. "The New Heat On Ford."
5. Reported by employee attending Alan Mulally's "Farewell Address" at Global Town Hall, Monday, June 23, 2014, at Ford Motor Company's World Headquarters Auditorium.
6. Kiley, David. "The New Heat On Ford."
7. Ibid.
8. Ibid.
9. Caldicott, Sarah Miller. "Why Alan Mulally Is An Innovation CEO..."
10. Saenz, Aaron. "MIT Unravels the Secrets Behind Collective Intelligence – Hint: IQ Not So Important." *Singularity Hub,* August 26, 2011. http://singularityhub.com/2011/08/26/mit-unravels-the-secrets-behind-collective-intelligence-hint-iq-not-so-important/.
11. Woolley, Anita Williams, Christopher F. Chabris, Alex Pentland, Nada Hashmi, and Thomas W. Malone. "Evidence for a Collective Intelligence Factor in the Performance of Human Groups." *Science* 330, no. 6004 (October 29, 2010): 686-88, doi: 10.1126/science.1193147.
12. Beilock, Sian. "What Predicts the Success of People Working Together to Solve a Problem? It's Not What You May Think." *Psychology Today,* November 4, 2014. http://www.psychologytoday.com/blog/choke/201011/what-predicts-the-success-people-working-together-solve-problem-it-s-not-what-you-.
13. Woolley, Anita Williams, Christopher F. Chabris, Alex Pentland, Nada Hashmi, and Thomas W. Malone. "Evidence for a Collective Intelligence Factor..."
14. Saenz, Aaron. "MIT Unravels the Secrets Behind Collective Intelligence..."
15. "Leading in the 21st century: An interview with Ford's Alan Mulally." *McKinsey & Company*
16. Ibid.

CHAPTER 2

1. Multiple sources.
2. The talented trainer Laura Fleming visited our offices in Denver, Colorado, and shared the concept in 2013.
3. Peavey, Fran. "Strategic Questioning: An Approach to Creating Personal and Social Change,." *ActiveDemocracy.net*, 1997. http://www.activedemocracy.net/articles/PeaveyStrategicQuestioning.pdf
4. Cooperrider, David L., and Diana Whitney. *Collaborating for Change: Appreciative Inquiry.* San Francisco, CA: Barrett-Koehler Communications, 1999.
   Trosten-Bloom, Amanda, and Diana Whitney. "Creative AI Approaches for Whole-System Culture Change: Hunter Douglas Window Fashions Division." *The Appreciative Inquiry Commons,* August 16, 2001. http://appreciativeinquiry.case.edu/intro/bestcasesDetail.cfm?coid=209. Arcoleo, Deborah. "Underneath Appreciative Inquiry: The Power of Positive Conversation." ODE master's thesis, *The Fielding Institute,* 2001.

CHAPTER 3

1. We are inspired and influenced by G. Hendrick's excellent book, *The Big Leap.* In it he uses the term "Upper-Limiting Problem" to describe the last obstacle a person needs to solve to be able to function in his or her "zone of genius." The High Performance Ceiling advances Hendrick's ideas into the team concept. Hendricks, Gay. *The Big Leap: Conquer Your Hidden Fear and Take Life to the Next Level.* New York: HarperCollins, 2008.
2. Blanding, Michael, "Pulpit Bullies: Why Dominating Leaders Kill Teams." *Harvard Business School, Working Knowledge.* November 18, 2013. http://hbswk.hbs.edu/item/7361.html.
3. Famously stated by Warren Bennis. Original source unknown.
4. "Team negotiation and perceptions of trustworthiness: The whole versus the sum of the parts" from *Group dynamics: Theory, Research, and Practice.* Vol. 12 (2), June 2009. As related on Eric Barker's blog, "Is a team only as strong as its weakest link?" *Barking Up The Wrong Tree.* March 29, 2010. http://www.bakadesuyo.com/2010/03/is-a-team-only-as-strong-as-its-weakest-link/.
5. Pentland, Alex. "The New Science of Building Great Teams." *Harvard Business Review, The Magazine.* April 2012. http://hbr.org/2012/04/the-new-science-of-building-great-teams.
6. Pentland, Alex. "The Hard Science of Teamwork." *Harvard Business Review, HBR Blog Network.* March 20, 2012. http://blogs.hbr.org/2012/03/the-new-science-of-building-gr/.
7. "McDonald's and Lafley's Letters to P&G Employees." *Cincinnati.com, A Gannett Company.* May 23, 2013. http://archive.cincinnati.com/article/20130523/BIZ01/305230259/McDonald-s-Lafley-s-letters-P-G-employees

CHAPTER 4

1. Famously stated by Peter Drucker. Original source unknown.
2. Goldsmith, Marshall, and Mark Reiter. *What Got You Here Won't Get You There: How Successful People Become Even More Successful.* New York: Hyperion, 2007.

Activation Point #5: "The Antidote To Communication Competition" was adapted from the Leadership Post "5 Signs You are In a Losing Game: Communication Competition," published March 2010.

Activation Point #7: "Why Are You Invited to Meetings?" was originally published under the same title, with slight revisions, October 2012.

Activation Point #9: "The War For Problem Talent" was adapted from the Leadership Post "The War for Problem Talent," published October 2012.

Activation Point #10: "The Most Important Decision Of A Career" was adapted from the Leadership Post of the same name, published January 2014.

CHAPTER 5

1. Collins, Jim, and Morten T. Hansen. *Great by Choice: Uncertainty, Chaos and Luck – Why Some Thrive Despite Them All*. New York: HarperCollins, 2011.
2. Wiseman, Liz, and Greg McKeown. *Multipliers: How The Best Leaders Make Everyone Smarter*. New York: HarperBusiness, 2010
3. Duhugg, Charles. *The Power of Habit: Why We Do What We Do in Life and Business*. New York: Random House, 2012

Activation Point #17: "When Playing It Safe Hurts" was adapted from the Leadership Post "How Playing it Safe Can Hurt," published January 2012.

Activation Point #18: "I Blowed It Up" was adapted from the Leadership Post "I Blowed It Up," published December 2007.

Activation Point #19: "Free Gas For Life" was adapted from the Leadership Post "Free Gas for Life," published August 2012.

CHAPTER 6

1. Burns, James MacGregor. *Leadership*. New York: Harper & Row, 1978.
2. Collins, Jim and Morten T. Hansen. *Great by Choice: Uncertainty, Chaos and Luck – Why Some Thrive Despite Them All*. New York: HarperCollins, 2011.
3. 180° Shift[SM] © 2008, Verus Global, Inc. All rights reserved.
4. *Respectfully Quoted: A Dictionary of Quotations Requested from the Congressional Research Service*. Washington, D.C.: Library of Congress, 1989; Bartleby.com, 2003. http://www.bartleby.com/73/2099.html.

Activation Point #28: "Data Rich, Knowledge Poor" was originally published as a Leadership Post in May, 2012.

Activation Point #30: "A Call For Certain Courage" was adapted from the Leadership Post of the same name, published March 2014.

Activation Point #31: "It Happens When You Elevate The Reason" was adapted from the Leadership Post of the same name, published February 2014.

CHAPTER 7

1. Bridges, William. *Managing Transitions: Making the Most of Change.* Reading, MA: Addison-Wesley, 1991.

Activation Point #32: "It's Not The Time, It's The Performance Paradigm" was adapted from the Leadership Post "The All-Time Most Common Excuse," originally published March 2010.

Activation Point #35: "How To Support Peers through Change" was adapted from Verus Global QuickRead "A Change for the Better," published 2012.

Activation Point #38: "One Word To Achieve More: No" was adapted from the Leadership Post "One Word to Execute Faster: No," originally published in October 2012.

Activation Point #40: "What It Takes To Be A Legend" was adapted from Leadership Post of the same name published March 2014.

CHAPTER 8

1. Dan Pink has done remarkable work on studying motivation. For more on this topic, we recommend this TED Talk: www.ted.com/talks/dan_pink_on_motivation.html and his book, *Drive*. Pink, Daniel H. *Drive: The Surprising Truth About What Motivates Us.* New York: Riverhead, 2011.

Activation Point #42: "What Causes Us To Give More" was adapted from Verus Global QuickRead "A Change for the Better," published 2012.

Activation Point #45: "The Michelangelo Approach To High Performance" was adapted from the Leadership Post "Are You the Michelangelo of Leadership? Take this Quiz." originally published October 2009.

Activation Point #49: "Do Bonuses Increase Engagement? (If Not, What Does?)" was adapted from the Leadership Post "of the same name, originally published August 2012.

CHAPTER 9

1. Schulz, Kathryn. "On Being Wrong." Filmed March 2011. TED video, 17:57. Posted April 19, 2011. http://blog.ted.com/2011/04/19/on-being-wrong-kathryn-schulz-on-ted-com/.

APPENDIX B

1. Famously stated by James A. Michener. Original source unknown.

INDEX

180° Shift, 133-134
3 Conditions that Accelerate Change, 198
3 Mind Factors, 127, 205
Accountability, 112, 166, 169-170
Achievementt, 114
Agility, 137
Alignment, 111-112, 135-136
All in, 175-176
Appreciative Inquiry, 44
Archimedes of Syracuse, 35
Attrition, 151, 154
Backward focus, 128, 133, 167, 235
Balance, 237
Behaviors, 68, 122, 241-242
Bennis, Warren, 16
Big 5 of Upstream Leadership, 137-138
Blame, 127
Blanding, Michael, 52
Bridges, William, 167
Bronc, 177-178
Burns, James, 129
Business model, 169
Capability, 108, 195
Capacity, 108
Carnegie Mellon University, 28
Casey Stengel, 3
Celebration, 207-208
Change, 167-168
Change model, 167-168
Co-Discover, 130
Collaboration, 115, 131-132
Collins, Jim, 133
Commitment, 150
Commitment, 175-176
Communication, 129-130
Community, 78
Competencies, 7-8, 68, 122

Complaining, 115
Concern, 219
Conflict, 99-100
Consensus, 131-132
Consequences, 163-164
Consistency, 241
Continuous improvement, 10, 81-82, 226
Conversation, 129-130
Cooperrider, David, 44
Courage, 103-104, 117, 143, 180
Culture, 67-68, 116, 136, 137, 146, 152, 154, 209-210
Cumings, e.e., 61
Customer, 17, 73-74, 218, 230, 241
Data, 139-140
Deadline, 220
Decision making, 139-140, 166, 241
Decisions, 197
Discipline, 163
Discretionary effort, 189
Discussion, 129-130
Diversity, 199-200
Drucker, Peter, 209
Empathy, 77-78
Empowerment, 107, 165
Endurance, 177-178
Energy Map, 127
Engagement, 203-204
Excellence, 115-116, 195-196, 208, 241
Execution, 63-64
Expectations, 116, 162
Failure, 165, 179-180, 207
Family, 77-78
Fear, 115, 167, 179-180, 219
Feedback, 205-206
Fire-fighting, 105
Focus, 113-114, 127-128, 130, 133-134, 205-206

Ford, 25-27, 32-33
Forward Focus, 36, 127-128, 167, 174, 196
Forward Focus Questions, 133, 154, 173-174
Friendship, 171-172
Frustration, 219
Goal, 137
Godin, Seth, 197
Grand Canyon, 231
Great by Choice, 133
Growth, 191
Habit, 123, 241-242
Hansen, Morten T., 133
High Performance Ceiling, 6, 49-52, 96, 106, 109, 113, 141, 150, 177, 227, 230, 239, 241
High Performance Discussion, 129-140, 163, 176
High Performance Strategy, 129-130, 197-198
Honesty, 65-66
Identity, 73-74
Inclusion, 75-76
Indecisiveness, 167
Influence, 229
Initiative, 115-116
Innovation, 101, 110, 145-146, 151
Inspiration, 144, 201-202, 232
Instincts, 101-102
Integrity, 143-144
Jigsaw puzzle, 239
Judgement, 117
Kennedy, John F., 13-15, 35, 44
Knowledge, 139-140
Lafley, A.G., 57-58
Leadership, 105, 152
Leading up, 235
Learn, 81-82
Legacy, 83-84
Listen, 130

Long Lever Question Feedback Form, 39, 245
Long Lever Questions, 36-39, 41-42, 45-47, 51, 54, 58, 89-91, 96, 123-125, 152-159, 179, 184-187, 215-216, 218-224, 227, 230, 232-233, 245
Losing, 207
Loyalty, 171-172
Managing up, 235
Manipulation, 6
Marshall Goldsmith, 69
Meetings, 76, 123
Menken, H. L., 161
Message, 129
Mexico City, 239
Michelangelo, 195-196, 231
Mindset, 99-100
Mistakes, 99, 105, 115-116
MIT, 28, 55
Model, 129
Momentum, 113-114
Motivation, 179-180, 236
Mulally, Alan, 25-28, 30, 32-33
Organizational chart, 58, 135
Ownership, 146, 152, 154
P&G, 57-58
Partnerships, 193-194
Peace Corps, 17
Peavey, Fran, 36
Pentland, Alex, 55-57
Performance, 191-192, 218
Performance reviews, 31
Perseverance, 99-100
Platform statement, 153
Politics, 135
Positioning statement, 153, 223-224
Potential, 12, 141, 155
Power, 4, 6
Pride, 189

Priorities, 162
Proactive, 197
Problems, 127
Productive paranoia, 134
Productivity, 135, 151
Professionalism, 65-66
PTO, 237
Quality, 145-146
Questions Trigger the Mind, 15
Refusal, 173-174
Rejection, 173-174
Relationships, 171, 193-194
Reorganization, 220, 232
Reputation, 109
Respect, 66, 117
Responsibility, 108, 170, 215-216
Results, 124
Reward, 110, 124
Risk analysis, 105
Risk-taking, 109-110
Rodeo, 177
Root-cause analysis, 105
Rumors, 220
Safety, 109
Schulz, Kathryn, 232
Shareholder, 136, 189, 191
Sistine Chapel, 231
Solutions, 127
Stack, Jack, 197
Stories, 189-190
Strategic thinking, 133
Strategy, 133
Success, 165, 207
Survival, 109
Systems, 239-240
Talent, 79-80
Team Activation Checklist, 137-138
Teamwork, 69-70, 233

The Great Game of Business, 197
The Last Judgement, 231
Time management, 161-162
Tough issues, 103
Traffic jam, 241
Transactional leadership, 129
Transformational leadership, 129
Transparency, 71-72, 153
Trust, 115, 135-136, 153, 209-210
Union College, 28
Vacation, 237
Value, 170
Values, 70, 141
Vision, 111, 141, 154
Whitney, Diana, 44
Winning, 207-208
Wiseman, Liz, 106
Work-life balance, 237